```
3 1146 00052 2544
```

```
D1507526
```

## DATE DUE

| | | March 2, 2005 |
|---|---|---|
| MAR 1 2 1997 | | |
| | | OCT 1 9 2006 |
| NOV 9 1997 | | NOV 0 3 2009 |
| MAY 2 9 1998 | | |
| MAR 2 1 1999 | | |
| NOV 2 1 1999 | | |
| APR 2 2 2000 | | |
| OCT 2 1 2003 | | |
| JUL 0 8 2004 | | |
| 090804 | | |
| JAN 2 5 2005 | | |
| FEB 1 6 2005 | | |

# THE IMAGE OF
# PUERTO RICO

# OTHER BOOKS
# BY ROBIN McKOWN

*Nonfiction*
THE CONGO, RIVER OF MYSTERY
THE AMERICAN REVOLUTION: THE FRENCH ALLIES
HEROIC NURSES
THE STORY OF THE INCAS
BENJAMIN FRANKLIN
THOMAS PAINE
MARIE CURIE
ROOSEVELT'S AMERICA
ELEANOR ROOSEVELT'S WORLD
WASHINGTON'S AMERICA
THE FABULOUS ISOTOPES
GIANT OF THE ATOM: ERNEST RUTHERFORD
SHE LIVED FOR SCIENCE: IRÈNE JOLIOT-CURIE
MENDELEYEV AND HIS PERIODIC TABLE
SEVEN FAMOUS TRIALS
THE MONGO HOMECOMING (with Mary Elting)
COLONIAL CONQUEST OF AFRICA
THE REPUBLIC OF ZAÏRE
LUMUMBA
NKRUMAH
CRISIS IN SOUTH AFRICA
THE WORLD OF MARY CASSATT

*Fiction*
THE BOY WHO WOKE UP IN MADAGASCAR
GIRL OF MADAGASCAR
RAKOTO AND THE DRONGO BIRD
THE ORDEAL OF ANNE DEVLIN
JANINE
PATRIOT OF THE UNDERGROUND

# THE IMAGE OF PUERTO RICO

Its History and its People:
on the Island — on the Mainland

## ROBIN McKOWN

McGraw-Hill Book Company
New York   St. Louis   San Francisco   Düsseldorf   Johannesburg
Kuala Lumpur   London   Mexico   Montreal   New Delhi   Panama
Rio de Janeiro   Singapore   Sydney   Toronto

# TO
# DOROTHY MARDFIN

## ACKNOWLEDGMENTS

Picture appearing on page 1, top left, courtesy of Rare Book Division, The New York Public Library, Astor, Lenox and Tilden Foundations.

Pictures appearing on page 1, top right and bottom, and page 2, top, courtesy of the New York Public Library.

Pictures appearing on page 2, bottom, and pages 4, 5, 6, 7, courtesy of the National Board of Puerto Rican Tourism.

Pictures appearing on page 3, courtesy of the National Archives.

Pictures appearing on page 8, courtesy of United Press International.

Library of Congress Cataloging in Publication Data

McKown, Robin.
The image of Puerto Rico.

SUMMARY: Traces the history of Puerto Rico from its discovery by Columbus to its future as a possible fifty-first state or independent nation.
1. Puerto Rico—Juvenile literature. [1. Puerto Rico] I. Title.
F1958.3.M27    972.95    72-13285
ISBN 0-07-045367-5 (lib. bdg.)

# CONTENTS

# FOREWORD

Robin McKown provides in *The Image of Puerto Rico* a felicitous narrative and a delightfully written cameo portrait of the Puerto Ricans and Puerto Rico.

Perhaps Robin McKown's success in dealing with so complex a phenomenon as a people, their culture and their history derives from the modesty with which she approached the task, and from the infectiously intuitive love (*tengo Puerto Rico en mi corazón*) that she has come to feel for the island and its people. In a letter to me she expressed these feelings thusly: "I had felt very uncertain about it [writing her book on Puerto Rico], myself. It had seemed to me that a non-Puerto Rican should not have attempted it. But you can probably guess that I fell deeply in love with your beautiful island and the people in my all too brief stay, and that I was fascinated with its colorful history, so little-known here." There is in Puerto Rican history and in the cultural/thematic ideals of her people the hauntingly continuing refrain of the sentiments which Robin McKown evokes. The Puerto Rican poet, José Gautier Benítez (1848–1880), best captures the intensity of its appeal in the apostrophic cadences addressed to the island:

> All that is in you is voluptuous and light
> Sweet, gentle, caressing and tender,
> And your moral world owes its enchantment
> To the sweet influence of your external world.

What Robin McKown has achieved is an essentially kaleidoscopic overview of the Puerto Rican experience on the island, and tangentially on the mainland. She has captured an elusive Puerto Rican *ethos,* and all without an element of controversy or intrusive insensitivity. Her narrative is a judicious distillation of history, sociology, anthropology, and political sovereignty, all objectively structured and lucidly articulated. And nowhere is this more clear than in her handling of the contemporary *Weltpolitik* which has witnessed a resurgent *independista* ideology *vis à vis* the continuing controversial Commonwealth status; she has, in the main, avoided the tractarian and ideological encounters which severely damage some of the books on Puerto Rico which have recently appeared as part of an evolving tendentious literature.

In a period when a knowledge of Puerto Ricans and Puerto Rico is vital to the well being of all Americans, Robin McKown's *The Image of Puerto Rico* is the best brief contemporary account in English, to be compared only with the superb brief history of José Luis Vivas, *Historia de Puerto Rico* (1962). And that is no small achievement.

FRANCESCO CORDASCO
City University of New York
Former Consultant
Migration Division
Commonwealth of Puerto Rico

# ▌ PUERTO RICANS
# ▌ ARE NOT FOREIGNERS

*"I am going back to Puerto Rico even if I have to go back swimming. There even just eating bananas I will go through life singing."*

*— Popular song*

Approximately 1,500,000 persons in the continental United States were born on the island of Puerto Rico or are the children of Puerto Rican parents, approaching half of the island's 2,800,000 population. During the 1950's, Puerto Ricans came to the mainland on an average of 45,000 a year. Most of them were in search of better jobs. Even the most menial work paid more than on their poor and overcrowded island.

Puerto Ricans have settled down in every state in the union. At least two-thirds of them, about one million, live in the five boroughs of New York City, mostly in the Bronx and Brooklyn, and in Manhattan's Spanish Harlem, which they call *El Barrio.* The influx of Spanish-speaking Puerto Ricans has given a new flavor to the city. There are cafés and restaurants called Borinquen,* the ancient Indian name for Puerto Rico. There is a Borinquen dry cleaning establishment, a Borinquen beauty salon, a Borinquen florist, and a night club called La Borinqueña.

Tins of Puerto Rican specialties are sold in the supermarkets. Spanish grocery stores (*bodegas*) sell plantains, large green bananas cooked as vegetables, and other Puerto Rican fruits and vegetables. A Spanish book store specializes in Puerto Rican literature. There is a Puerto Rican traveling theater. One hears Spanish in the subways, in the parks, everywhere. In public

* *Originally spelled Boriquén.*

schools, where one out of four children is Puerto Rican, some special classes have been set up to teach them English. And efforts are being made in bilingual education (Spanish and English). Admittedly, such programs are insufficient. Many Puerto Rican children fall behind because of language difficulties.

Puerto Rico is a Commonwealth of the United States and thus all Puerto Ricans are American citizens. As citizens, they can travel to the mainland without passports, visas, or any customs formalities. They have indeed as much right to move to New York as a New Yorker has to settle down in Nebraska—or to take a vacation in Puerto Rico.

Some of them have become famous. Among those whom everyone knows are actor José Ferrer, opera singer Graciela Rivera, actress Rita Moreno, boxers José Torres, Carlos Ortiz, and Sixto Escobar. There was also baseball player Roberto Clemento, who died on a mercy mission. Representative Herman Badillo of New York became the first Puerto Rican with a vote in Congress. Puerto Ricans have been elected as senators and assemblymen in the New York State legislature. A Puerto Rican, Joseph Monserrat, was appointed president of the New York City Board of Education; an increasing number of Puerto Ricans are serving as educators and teachers in the city schools.

Many Puerto Ricans have attended mainland universities. They have taken degrees as doctors, lawyers, architects, engineers. Some have stayed on to make their careers among the "Continentales"—as Puerto Ricans call Americans on the continent. Many others have returned to join their fellow professionals on the island.

Yet, for every Puerto Rican family that has achieved middle-class living standards or above, there are ten or twenty or more who are entangled in "the poverty level." An estimated half of the Puerto Ricans in New York are on welfare, an even larger percentage than the black population, not because they will not take any work they can get, but because they have no alternative.

Puerto Ricans have not been made welcome in the States. They have met hostility rather than hospitality. Those with dark skins have had to cope with the slights and slurs that Afro-Americans endured for so long. Puerto Ricans, whatever the color of their skin, have suffered job discrimination, been refused work for which they were equipped, been paid less than their fellow Americans, ignored by some unions, treated with contempt by those who should know better. They have been subjected to all sorts of nonsense from prejudiced, ill-informed, insecure, or vicious people, who have convinced themselves that anyone who does not speak English—or speaks it with an accent—belongs to a lower order of the human race.

They have had immense difficulty finding decent housing. Exuberant by nature, they have been confined to small and dismal apartments in the city slums or, at best, sterile housing projects, not an atmosphere to keep young people at home. Non-English-speaking mothers, timid and bewildered, watch helplessly as their children run wild on the streets; join gangs; take up smoking, drinking, drugs; get into trouble with the police. Nor do the fathers have the same authority they do in Puerto Rico. In Puerto Rico, a man's children obey him without question. In the States, with his awkward English and low income status, he is frequently no longer master of his own household.

Many well-meaning persons have given a great deal of attention to the "Puerto Rican problem"—social workers, sociologists, priests, teachers, politicians. They have done some good but, all too often, their efforts are marred by a patronizing attitude. Puerto Ricans, no more than anyone else, do not like to be patronized. They like it less and less as time goes on. They do not think of themselves as a problem. In fact, it occurs to many of them that the people who treat them so nastily are the problem.

Early in 1969, a group of Puerto Rican New York City college students formed an organization dedicated to fighting for better conditions for their people. At first, they called themselves the Society of Albizu Campos, after Puerto Rico's most militant advocate for independence. Later, they took the more appealing name of Young Lords Party.

Most of the Young Lords had grown up in New York's Spanish

Harlem or in the slums of Chicago. Some of them had taken drugs, been involved in petty crime, spent time in reform schools or jails. Unlike the social workers and other well-intentioned outsiders, they were part and parcel of the Puerto Rican community and knew firsthand the evils that poverty and privation can breed.

It seemed to these young men that the first thing on their agenda must be to find some activity that would bring New York Puerto Ricans together in a common cause—that only by unity could they advance. One hot, summer Sunday they descended on Spanish Harlem with brooms and began to sweep the garbage from the sidewalks and streets. They wore berets and large buttons which read, "All Power to the People."

Their fellow Puerto Ricans thought at first that the Mayor had sent them. They also suspected them of being Communists. But by the third Sunday of garbage sweeping, people began to accept them. Some of them helped cleaning up the streets. When their brooms wore out, the Young Lords went to the city Sanitation Department and asked for more. They were turned down. In official quarters, their labors were clearly not appreciated.

That October, the Young Lords asked a Methodist church to give them space to serve breakfast to poor children. The Church Board voted an arbitrary no. The Young Lords went through all the proper channels to get them to reverse their decision, but none of their pleas were heeded. Finally, they simply occupied the church, peacefully and without guns, but with the efficiency of a military operation. Once in charge, they not only served breakfast to poor children but launched on other community activities. They conducted a free health program, a day care center, gave political education classes, ran a drive to collect clothing, and held poetry readings in the evening.

Newspapers found them excellent copy. They were invited to appear on television. When, after eleven days, the police evicted them from the church, public sympathy everywhere was with the Young Lords.

The Young Lords Party grew rapidly. They set up branches in other cities. All-male at first, the Party began admitting girls—for typing, making coffee, and other routine tasks. Under indirect influence of the woman's liberation movement, women were later allowed to serve as organizers and executives. Another task the Young Lords undertook was to try to patch up the often bitter differences between Puerto Ricans and Afro-Americans and to work jointly with them as another oppressed minority.

Inevitably, there were some stodgy stuffed shirts who fumed and fussed about the Young Lords, but, on the whole, their imaginative exploits went a long way toward creating a new image of the Puerto Rican people on the continent. They restored to Puerto Ricans here their *dignidad* (their dignity), which at home has always been of supreme importance to them, rating higher than money or power or worldly success. The Young Lords have also led the way for other Puerto Rican organizations aimed to give their people their proper place in American society, with as much right to protest the war in Vietnam or other matters they consider unjust and unfair as any other Americans.

Compared to the early European immigrants, whose voyage to America took weeks, Puerto Ricans live but a stone's throw away. The jet air flight takes a mere 3 hours; an economy flight from 12 P.M. to 3 A.M. costs but seventy-five dollars round trip. Over the last two decades, Puerto Ricans have grown very nonchalant about air travel. They usually manage to find money to go home for holidays or to visit their families. They invite relatives to come visit them. In off-seasons, Puerto Rican sugar-cane workers arrive as migrant laborers for specified periods, many under contract.

This constant coming and going makes it hard to find out how many Puerto Ricans reside *permanently* on the mainland, but one thing is certain. Beginning in the late '60's, more Puerto Ricans have returned to Puerto Rico than have left it.

This movement back to the island somehow coincides with the rise of Puerto Rican civil rights groups. While some stay on and fight, others simply give up. One Spanish-speaking Puerto Rican left after the police picked him up for a crime he had not committed and put him through a nightmare ordeal to prove his innocence. Many Puerto Rican families have moved back to the island because, while juvenile delinquency is increasing there, it is nowhere near the threat it is on mainland U. S. A. The rise in unemployment has also hit the Puerto Rican population harder than other segments of the mainland population.

Perhaps, the main reason for going home is pure homesickness for the blue skies and sunny climate of the island. If anything holds Puerto Ricans together on the mainland, it is their fierce loyalty to their own land, a loyalty that grows more intense in the years of exile. The sad thing is that so few of them have ever had a chance to become part of the life of the continent, have ever known—as friends and companions—their fellow, English-speaking American citizens. It is equally true, and equally unfortunate, that in an atmosphere thick with prejudice, not many mainlanders learn anything of the background of their Puerto Rican colleagues. It would seem that only a trip to Puerto Rico could fill such a gap.

# 2 AMERICA'S TROPICAL PLAYGROUND

*"I have broken the rainbow*
*against my heart . . .*
*I have blown the clouds of rose color and blood color*
*beyond the farthest horizons*
*I have drowned my dreams."*
— Luis Muñoz Marín

For visitors from the States, the island of Puerto Rico is a vacation in paradise, a tropical playground.

In Puerto Rico, flaming poinsettias grow 16 feet tall. They frame the veranda in the ultramodern mansion of the prosperous executive. They embrace the simplest dwelling of the farm worker. They grow wild along the roadside.

In Puerto Rico, people claim that if you break off a branch, stick it in the ground, and press the soil down firmly with your heel, the branch will take root, sprout green leaves, and burst into bloom. Gardens are a medley of flowering plants and ornamental bushes—hibiscus, gardenia, bougainvillea, jasmine, oleander, golden trumpet, cup of gold, the Maltese cross—so called because the petals of its bright, red flowers have the shape of a cross—and the lovely queen-of-the-night, whose pale fragrant blossoms open only after dark.

Flowering trees are part of the Puerto Rican landscape—some native, some imported from Asia, from Africa, from all over. There is the African tulip tree, the frangipani, the silk cotton tree, the violet tree—native to Puerto Rico, which, in the spring, is covered with tiny violet blossoms—and the flamboyant from Madagascar, which, during its long blooming season, turns country roads into scarlet-lined tunnels.

There are banana trees of many kinds; orange trees which shade the coffee plants on steep mountain slopes; lime, lemon, and grapefruit trees; mango and papaya trees with large, shiny, decorative leaves; breadfruit from Tahiti; cashew trees and avocados. A large avocado and a loaf of bread are a meal for many poor families.

There are, of course, palms. The first impression of a stranger from wintry New York, stepping from his plane in the warm Puerto Rican dusk, will be what seems a mirage—a row of tall palm trees outlined against a sunset sky.

The stranger's second impression, on his taxi ride into San Juan, Puerto Rico's capital, will make him feel he is back home—a massive traffic jam on a many-lane highway. Industrialization in Puerto Rico has proceeded faster than in other Caribbean islands, with inevitable side effects. Coastal highways near the major cities are crowded with trucks and lined with factories, billboards, junkyards, shopping centers, supermarkets, used car lots. Happily, a large part of the island is still unspoiled.

In Puerto Rico, at night, the countryside resounds with the song of a miniature tree frog, the *coqui*. "Coqui-qui-qui-qui," he sings, sometimes in chorus with hundreds of companions. It is said that once you have heard the refrain of coqui, it will haunt you forever.

In Puerto Rico, there is rarely a day when the sun does not shine. Patriots claim that Puerto Rican sky is of a deeper blue than other lands and that the clouds are whiter. Temperatures, from 70° to 80° F, are never cold, seldom too hot. Only in the mountains are evenings cool enough for a sweater.

Puerto Rico is the setting of numerous scenic wonders. One of them is Phosphorescent Bay, near the fishing village of Parguera. Here, large populations of a tiny form of marine life called dinoflagellates produce luminescent sparks when disturbed. The wake of a boat is stitched with light. Drops of water cascade from leaping fish like iridescent waterfalls. A stone thrown into the bay causes a burst of sparks.

Puerto Rico's strange and forbidding *Karst country*, refers to areas where water has, over long periods, dissolved limestone rocks and produced a maze of caves, steep haystack hills, and deep conical holes. Most karst country is inaccessible, but near Arecibo, a huge karst sinkhole, more than 1300 feet across and almost a perfect circle, has been put to use for science. In it, the Arecibo Ionospheric Observatory, which operates the largest radar-radio telescope in the world, has installed a gigantic steel mesh reflector. Scientists of many nations come here to study the earth's ionosphere, the solar system, and the galaxies beyond.

A most enchanting part of Puerto Rico is El Yunque Rain Forest, named after the 3496-foot-high mountain El Yunque. This 28,000-acre stretch of jungles, hills, streams, and waterfalls, a bare hour's drive from San Juan, is the only rain forest in the West Indies and the only tropical preserve of the United States National Park Service. Here, giant ferns unfurl feathery branches up to 30 feet. Orchids in pastel shades cling to their host trees. Among the 200 species of trees are still hardwoods which, elsewhere, were cut down centuries before to build Spanish cathedrals, forts, monasteries, and homes. One of these is the mighty *ausubo*, called the bullet wood tree because of the toughness of its wood.

A combination of winds and mountains have made El Yunque the island's area of heaviest rainfall; it has an estimated 1600 showers a year, usually violent but brief. A combination of rainfall and rich soil is responsible for its lush greenery.

The island of Puerto Rico is 1040 miles from Miami and 1662 miles southeast of New York City. The Atlantic bounds it on the north and the Caribbean Sea on the south. It is the furthest east of the four major Caribbean islands of the Greater Antilles. The others are Cuba, Jamaica, and Hispaniola (divided between Haiti and the Dominician Republic). Puerto Rico, with an area of 3,423 square miles, is the smallest (little more than one-fifteenth the size of Cuba, with 44,218 square miles). It is the only island of the four not wholly independent. The Greater Antilles, together with the Windwards and Leewards and other small islands of the Lesser Antilles, were all once the high, mountainous regions of a long-sunken continent.

Roughly rectangular, Puerto Rico is 100 miles from east to west and 35 miles from north to south. The mountains of the interior—the Sierra de Luquillo and the Cordillera Central—are so steep they look in places like inverted ice cream cones. The highest is Cerro de Punto, 4398 feet above sea level. The beaches along Puerto Rico's more than 600 miles of coastline are superb. Crescent-shaped Luquillo Beach, which is edged by a coconut grove and has a mountain background, is advertised as the most beautiful in the Caribbean, a claim, to be sure, that other Caribbean islands make about their beaches.

Quite a few Americans from the continent have settled in Puerto Rico, retired people; doctors, or dentists, or professors who find they can make almost as good a living as at home; employees or executives of large American industries with Puerto Rican branches. There is also beginning to be an influx of Afro-Americans, enticed both by the scenery and the lack of racial discrimination. Living in Puerto Rico has some of the charm of living in a foreign country, but with the convenience of American money, American postage stamps, American banks.

A great effort has been made in the last decades to attract rich tourists. For a while, they came in great numbers. They lived in the luxury hotels built to accommodate them along Condado Beach in San Juan and elsewhere on the island. They came to sunbathe, to get a winter tan.

The sports-minded have a choice of swimming, snorkling, scuba diving, surfing, water skiing, yachting—or they can play tennis and golf. For playboy types, there are casinos where they can gamble—legally—and night clubs where they can sip drinks, and dance, and watch performers, who, more often than not, come from the mainland—brought over with the odd reasoning that tourists prefer shows such as they watch at home. The gourmet can dine at expensive French, Italian, Swiss, Japanese, or Chinese restaurants. Plain American food such as hot dogs and hamburgers is available. And, of course, for the adventurous, there are Puerto Rican restaurants serving the local cuisine—combinations of chicken, seafood, rice, and special spices—which epicures find delicious.

The tourist mecca, for sightseeing and for souvenirs, is Old San Juan, a mini-island in San Juan harbor on Puerto Rico's northern coast. Old San Juan, connected with the large and sprawling American-modern, new San Juan on Puerto Rico's mainland, dates back to 1521 and is the oldest city on American soil. Roughly triangular, it encompasses about seven city blocks, with some streets too narrow for traffic. To step into Old San Juan is to go back several centuries to a world of Spanish colonial mansions with grilled balconies, brass-studded doors, black-and-white tiled floors, beamed ceilings, and inner patios. (Some of them are now museums, art galleries, and book stores.) The numerous plazas are the same as in colonial times except that their trees are more ancient and gnarled.

Puerto Ricans say they can always recognize tourists visiting Old San Juan. They carry cameras, binoculars, tourist brochures with maps which they frequently open up and study, and a raffia bag with "Puerto Rico" in pink yarn across it—purchased at the first souvenir shop they entered—to carry more souvenirs. If they get lost, they ask directions in English or grammar-school Spanish, speaking very slowly and clearly as though to deaf children.

Old San Juan offers several spectacular guided tours. Two of them are through the labyrinths of the ancient forts of El Morro and San Cristóbal, where literate bilingual guides give a running commentary and tourists with a sense of humor can take photographs of each other on a heap of cannonballs. A third is through beautiful La Forteleza, a white building of mixed Spanish and Moorish architecture built in the sixteenth century as a fort and which, ever since, has been the residence of Puerto Rico's governors—for Spanish ones, then American governors, and today, Puerto Rican governors.

Puerto Rico's other major towns also have luxury hotels for wealthy tourists and attractions for sightseers. Ponce, on the southern coast and next largest after San Juan, is noted for its plaza with trees trimmed with mathematical precision in the shape of giant mushrooms; for the *Parque de Bombas* (firehouse), a joke of a building in red and black stripes with green and yellow trim, formerly a kiosk for an 1893 fair; and for the Museum of Ponce, built in ultramodern style by architect Edward Durrell Stone (who also did New York City's Museum of Modern Art). The European collection is a rather dull assortment of second-rate artists or second-rate paintings by first-rate artists, but there are regular showings of Puerto Rican and other Caribbean artists, which are frequently exciting and original, as well as a fascinating collection of Indian artifacts. The Museum was a gift to Ponce by her most celebrated citizen, Luis A. Ferré, millionaire industrialist who became Puerto Rico's governor.

For Puerto Ricans, Ponce is known as the cradle of liberty. The first organized movements for civil rights, for abolition of slavery, and for independence from the Spanish Crown took place here.

The third largest city of Puerto Rico is Mayagüez on the western coast—also Spanish colonial with flashes of modernity—the site of two rum distilleries and a brewery and a tropical garden said to have the largest assortment of exotic plants and trees in the Western Hemisphere. Historic San Germán on the southwest coast, which was repeatedly raided by French privateers in the sixteenth century, has a lovely seventeenth-century church, the Porta Coeli, now a museum of religious art. Barranquitas, in the mountains, is famous as the birthplace of the patriot Luis Muñoz Rivera, father of Luis Muñoz Marín, Puerto Rico's first elected governor. (In Spanish-speaking countries, children take their mother's family name as their own last name. "Marín" was the family name of Governor Muñoz' mother.)

Puerto Rico, an island itself, has a host of island satellites. Vieques, 3 by 21 miles, discovered by Columbus, has fine isolated beaches—the delight of shell collectors—and a cave in which it is said are still hidden ceremonial objects of an Indian chieftain who was killed by a Spaniard. The roar in the cave is reportedly his voice, warning white men to keep away.

Culebra, about 11 miles square, is mostly occupied by the U. S. Navy. A feud exists between Navy officials and its some 700 inhabitants. They have objected to the island being used as a gunnery practice area and for underwater demolitions which have wiped out a large coral reef, killed large numbers of lobsters and small fish, and threatened the livelihood of island fishermen.

Mona, 6 by 4½ miles, has cliffs 200 feet high and is honeycombed with caves and underground passages—hideouts of pirates and smugglers 3 centuries ago. Many local people claim they have seen the ghost of *El Portugués,* one of the most notorious of the outlaws.

It is not difficult for tourists to arrange trips to all these showplaces of Puerto Rico, especially if they have the means to rent a car, but on the whole, they meet few Puerto Ricans except for guides, waiters, and clerks in souvenir shops. The formidable façades of the splendid hotels built to attract them to Puerto Rico also serve to isolate them from the Puerto Rican people, as effectively as the wall of prejudice on the mainland. It is a pity. Travelers of olden times learned that the most enriching part of their travels was getting acquainted with people of other cultures and other customs, a lesson that has too often been forgotten in the modern age of jet flights and packaged tours.

Puerto Rico is not merely an American playground. As the home of some 2,800,000 people, it is more densely populated than any part of the United States except Rhode Island and New Jersey. Predominantly Spanish, their blood has mingled with persons of other nations and other races. Technically Americans, they are closer to Europeans in many ways than to Americans from Kansas, California, or Connecticut and closer to their Caribbean neighbors in other ways than to either Europe or mainland America.

There are rich Puerto Ricans and poor ones. There are Puerto Rican statesmen, lawyers, doctors, athletes, poets, musicians, artists, mountaineers, factory and farm workers and fishermen, and almost any other profession or trade you can name. They are a hospitable people who in the past made welcome refugees, escaped slaves, and shipwrecked sailors. They are noted for their wild humor and their zestful, emotional, turbulent nature, although such generalizations do not apply to all. They are a gentle, peaceful people too who, in the past, have turned to violence only under extreme pressure. Their past, which is being rediscovered by Puerto Rican historians and archaeologists and re-interpreted from a Puerto Rican rather than colonial viewpoint, is extraordinarily fascinating. Mainland Americans can profit by knowing them and their island better.

# 3 A DISCOVERY OF CHRISTOPHER COLUMBUS

*"All of these islands are very handsome and of very good
earth, but this one seemed to everybody the best."*
— *Shipmate of Columbus, speaking of Puerto Rico*

Admiral Christopher Columbus—Cristóbal Colón in Spanish—discovered Puerto Rico, not on his first and most famous voyage to the New World in 1492, but on his second voyage the next year.

On his first voyage, he stopped in the Bahamas, in Cuba, and in Hispaniola, annexing them all in the name of the Spanish Crown. Convinced he was nearing India, he called the island populations Indians.

On his return to Spain, Columbus displayed to his sponsors, King Ferdinand and Queen Isabella, a rare collection of mementos—strange and delicious fruits, brilliantly colored birds, trinkets of gold, along with several Indians. The royal couple were so impressed they backed Columbus' second voyage far more lavishly than the first.

Instead of three small ships (the Niña, Pinta, and Santa Maria), Columbus now commanded a seventeen-ship fleet. His crew and passengers totaled 1200 men, including astronomers, mapmakers, artisans, and laborers. Among the ship's officers were his son, Diego Columbus, and a 33-year-old veteran of the Spanish Moorish wars, Juan Ponce de León. Columbus' own diary of this second voyage has been lost. What is known about it comes from his son; from the fleet surgeon, Diego Alvarez Chanca; from the Spanish Priest, Father Bartolomé las Casas, who was not present but who had access to records now missing.

Columbus was under instructions to start colonies on his islands. For this purpose, he took along a good supply of European seeds and plants, especially wheat and sugar cane, as well as horses, donkeys, cattle, pigs, sheep, goats, dogs, and fowl. Personally, he was more interested in exploration. He and his crew sailed further south than before, looking for new islands.

On November 3, 1493, 39 days after leaving Spain, they sighted a small island which Columbus named Dominica, because it was Sunday (*domingo* in Spanish). He had found the Lesser Antilles. A larger island which they sighted a few days later was christened Santa María de Guadalupe. When it later became a French possession, its spelling was changed to Guadeloupe.

The people on Guadalupe or Guadeloupe were the Caribs, after whom the Caribbean Sea is named. By nature, they were militant, suspicious of the white strangers, independent, and adventurous. On occasion, they ate human flesh. Habitually, they raided other islands where the peaceful and home-loving Arawaks, or Tainos, lived. A group of Arawaks, twelve women and two men, approached Columbus and his men when they landed, making it known that they were captives of the Caribs and that they came from an island to the west called Boriquén. (Over the centuries, this native name for Puerto Rico has also been spelled Borenquen, Buriquen, Burenquen, and so on). Columbus agreed to take them to their home if they would show the way.

The fleet continued in a northwest direction. They passed several more islands. Near one of them, the Spaniards had their first encounter with the Caribs; one Spaniard was killed and another was wounded by their poison arrows. Shortly afterward, the Spaniards found themselves among a great mass of tiny islands. Columbus named them, altogether, the Eleven Thousand Virgins. They are today's Virgin Islands.

On November 18, the fleet reached a lovely little island set like an emerald in the blue sea. Columbus called it Gratiosa for the mother of a friend; he had promised to find her "a noble island." Today, it has reverted to its native name of Vieques (meaning crab)—and is part of the Commonwealth of Puerto Rico.

From Vieques, Columbus sighted a somewhat larger island about 10 miles to the west. They approached it the next morning, November 19, which to Puerto Ricans is Discovery Day, a national holiday. Their Indian passengers cried out with delight, saying this was Boriquén. At least two of the women and one boy were so excited they jumped overboard and swam to shore. After claiming the island for the Spanish Crown, Columbus christened it San Juan Bautista (St. John the Baptist). Decades later, the English still referred to it as St. John.

For the near 13 hours of daylight, the fleet cruised west, parallel to a barrier reef along the island's southern coast. From their ships, the men could see the rich, green fields of the coastal plains and the equally green mountains rising steeply beyond them. Because the wind was fresh, they did not try to land. By nightfall, they had sailed the entire 100-mile length of the island. They anchored at Cabo Rojo (Red Cape), at the extreme southwest.

The following morning, November 20, the fleet sailed northerly along Puerto Rico's western shore, hugging the coast and searching for a harbor where they could land and stock up on water and wood for galley fires. There is still intensive debate as to where that west coast landing was made. Was it Boquerón Bay in the south? Was it Aguada Bay far to the north? Or Mayagüez harbor, site of Puerto Rico's third largest city? Or was it, as the American historian Samuel Eliot Morison and the Puerto Rican historian Dr. Aurelio Tió both seem to think, at Añasco Bay, a little more than halfway up that western coast?

Local patriotism is involved in this ancient dispute. Each harbor town has gathered its own "proofs" that Columbus landed there. The matter will likely never be settled.

In whatever harbor they chose, the fleet spent 2 days, which must have been joyous for everyone. The men found plenty of water, wood, and fruit. Everyone went fishing. They caught sardines, shad, and bullhead among other species of fish, certainly a welcome change in their diet. One can assume that the air was warm and the sky as deeply blue as it is today.

They had the beach all to themselves. Not a single native appeared. One group of sailors ventured inland and found "a very big and fair house abandoned." The roof of the house was of growing grass and other greenery, they reported. They were reminded of "the garden arbors of Valencia." Twelve smaller houses were built around this large one. They too were empty. A pathway led from the houses to the bay.

The men judged that the big house was a summer residence for some very important citizen. They were wrong. They had discovered a coastal village, whose population had fled, probably to the mountains, at the sight of the strange ships with sails.

At daybreak, on November 22, the fleet quit Puerto Rican shores, heading for Hispaniola, where Columbus had left his first tiny colony. A short distance out to sea they passed Mona Island, like Vieques now a part of Puerto Rico. They did not see Culebra nor make note of any other of the miniature islands that dot the coastal waters.

A statue of Cristóbal Colón, high on a pedestal and holding aloft a cross, stands in the beautiful tree-bordered Plaza de Colon in Old San Juan. Other towns throughout the island have their own statues of him, including, of course, all those who claim that Columbus landed there. Though he visited Puerto Rico only once, and that briefly, for Puerto Ricans he remains a very special kind of hero. After all, they can point out, this Italian-born navigator in the employ of Spain never did touch the shores of mainland United States, nor even catch a glimpse of North America. It is reasonable that they should feel closer to him than the mainlanders do.

# 4 THE ARAWAKS
# OF BORIQUÉN

*"Borinquen is the daughter...of the sea and the sun."*
*—Popular song*

The Arawak people—sometimes called the Tainos—who occupied the island of Boriquén when Columbus arrived, had originally come from Venezuela. The Arawakan culture, to which they belonged, was the largest linguistic family of the Americas. Like other American Indians, including their relatives the Caribs, their ancestors crossed the Bering Straits from Asia, many thousands of years before when a land bridge stretched across the Straits. At least, this is the generally accepted theory of how the Americas were first populated.

The Arawaks were not Puerto Rico's first inhabitants. Before them, dating back, perhaps, as far as 200 B.C., the Igneri Indians occupied Puerto Rico. They are known for their paper-thin pottery with an exquisite white glaze, the finest ever found on the island. Centuries before them, people referred to now only as "archaic Indians" lived in caves around Loiza Aldea in the north. The mysteries surrounding these early peoples remain impenetrable. Contemporary Spanish accounts tell a great deal about the Arawaks.

Although early Spanish artists made them all look like unclothed Spanish ladies and gentlemen, even giving the men mustaches and pointed beards, they resembled Europeans no more than any other American Indians. Their skin was bronze, bronze-gold, or ivory. They had high cheekbones and full lips. Their hair was straight and black, and their larger dark eyes were set wide apart. They were smaller than the Spaniards but more lithe in their movements and exceedingly clean; they bathed several times a day. Early Spaniards spoke often of their great beauty.

Married women wore a square of cloth secured to their waist by a cord. For beauty, and probably for protection from mosquitoes and other insects, people painted their bodies in designs of black, white, and red. Both men and women adorned themselves with necklaces, bracelets, and legbands of shell, bone, or, more rarely, of gold, the only metal they knew. Village chieftains wore headdresses of red, blue, and yellow feathers. The tropical climate made other attire unnecessary. The heavy armor, helmets, and boots which the Spaniards habitually wore could have sent them into gales of laughter.

They lived in villages along the coast or in inland valleys near the rivers. Somehow, they sensed that they should stay clear of mosquito-breeding swamps. The first Spanish colonists were not so clever and suffered heavy casualties from malaria and yellow fever.

Long before the Spaniards came, the Arawaks had developed farming techniques. To plant cassava, the men made holes with a digging stick in the center of mounds of earth which they spaced in long rows. The women followed them and placed a piece of cassava root in each hole, which they covered with soil. Cassava was used for bread and, with corn, which they also cultivated, to make an alcoholic drink for festive occasions. They grew other root vegetables, as well as chili and garlic. The stone mortars and pestles with which they pounded corn or cassava to make flour are now avidly sought by collectors.

Native fruit trees—papaya, guava, mamey, higüera—and pineapples—furnished their sweets. They did not have oranges, lemons, limes, grapefruit, mangoes, bananas, or coconut palms which, with wheat, barley, and sugar cane were brought in by the Spaniards. Tobacco, still unknown in Europe, was smoked and used as a powderlike incense in religious ceremonies. (In Europe, tobacco quickly became popular—as the "Holy Curative Plant of the

Indies." Learned doctors recommended it for headaches, sores, broken limbs, goiter, the plague, and the common cold.)

The Arawaks were skilled fishermen, using nets and traps. For ocean fishing, they went out in their sturdy canoes. Along the river banks, they sometimes sprinkled narcotic plants which caused the fish to lose consciousness. They collected clams and snails on the seashore. Shellfish were an important part of their diet. The shells served both for adornment and utensils. They captured sea turtles when they came ashore to deposit their eggs.

The Arawaks were also hunters, using arrows with points of sharks' teeth, sharpened shells, fish fins, or bones. Although Puerto Rico then, as now, had no large animals, they could track wild rabbits, wood rats, agoutis (a rodent the size of a rabbit), and iguanas (a large lizard considered a special delicacy). With stones or harpoons, they went after the huge aquatic mammal, the manatee or sea cow. They had domesticated dogs, called *josibis*, who went with them on their hunt. These dogs are now extinct.

The Arawak homes, called *bohios*, were usually round and built of palm trunks, lashed together with fibers, covered with palm bark or leaf sheaves, and roofed with straw. The floors were raised on posts as protection against floods. The word bohio was later applied to the shacks of Puerto Rico's poor, made of scrap boards and flattened tin cans or other castoff materials; they too were raised off the ground.

The hammock was their chief article of furniture. Everyone knows how popular this West Indian invention became with sailors at sea. Woven baskets were containers for personal possessions. From clay, the Arawaks made earthen vessels, pots and cooking pans, jars, and large plates from which they ate—decorated in geometric designs or figures representing their gods or mythological creatures. They made tools and trays from mahogany.

Of special interest to archaeologists are the statues which they carved of wood, modeled of clay, or cut from stone and marble. Some of their human figures had the oblique, slanted eyes of the Mongolians. Others portrayed men who were part ape, snakes with human faces, oddly distorted frogs. Some of these curios are to be seen in the museum at Ponce.

The Arawaks were accomplished musicians. Their song, *Borinqueña*, was a recitation with complicated rhythms of considerable sophistication, accompanied by the *maguey* (a small wooden drum), and the *maracas* (rattles made of gourds). Pageants and dances supplemented the music in a sort of operatic production.

The chief of each village was called the *cacique*. Both as a ruler and a judge, he had absolute power. His post was hereditary, but when he died, it was the son of his sister, not his own son, who replaced him. Each village had its quota of warriors who were known as *nitainos* and had special privileges. Also highly placed were the *bohiques*, who were priests and doctors combined. The *nabori* were the workers, who tilled soil, made tools, hunted, fished, and fought when required. Property was held in common. No one thought of trying to collect more possessions than he could use. Stealing was unknown.

Each village had two main streets which crossed in a public square called the *batey*. The cacique's house, which was rectangular and had a shaded porch, faced the batey. Other small, round houses crowded the main streets and alleys off the main streets.

All village activities took place in the batey—meetings, military drill, games, and dances. Religious rites were held in sacred places far from the villages. In certain parts of Puerto Rico are level spaces enclosed by rings of stones. The most important of these is near Utuado in the mountains. Constructed in the thirteenth century, it covers about 13 acres, has paved walks, plazas, and long parallel lines of standing stones, some carved in relief with figures, possibly of gods. Puerto Ricans have named this the Indian Ceremonial Ball Park; it is believed that the Arawaks gathered here under the cacique Guarionex for a combination of ball games and religious ceremonies.

The people of Boriquén worshiped a spirit of good and feared a spirit of evil, who might be compared to the Christian God and devil. For them, life did not end with death. The deceased became *jupias* and lived on in secluded parts of the island, resting by day and eating wild fruits and visiting their living neighbors at night. Until Columbus discovered their island, the raiding Caribs were the only danger the Arawaks knew. For a while, they thought that the bearded strangers in their great sailing ships had come to protect them from the Caribs.

Spain, at first, ignored the island Columbus had named San Juan Bautista. A nobleman named Vicente Yañez Pinzón was finally commissioned to conquer and colonize it. He visited the island briefly in 1499, then returned to Spain. In 1506, the year Columbus died, Pinzón transferred his rights to Martín Garcia de Zalazar. Neither of these first Spanish "governors" of Puerto Rico seem to have done more than land a few goats and hogs.

Juan Ponce de Léon, who had accompanied Columbus on his second voyage and stayed on in Hispaniola, was granted permission by Nicolás de Ovando, Governor of all the West Indies, to start a colony of his own in Puerto Rico. On August 12, 1508, he landed in the bay of Guanica, on the southern coast with an escort of fifty men and his interpreter, Juan González. Ponce de León was one of the soldier-explorer-colonizers in the wake of Columbus' discoveries now known as *conquistadors* (conquerors). They were men of great bravery and physical stamina. They loved adventure for its own sake. They were also greedy for gold and ruthless; they used their adherence to Christianity as a shield to hide horrible misdeeds. One word describes their treatment of the Indians, both in the Caribbean and on the mainland—treacherous. Ponce seems to have been only a little more humane than his brother conquistadors.

The Indians of Guanica welcomed him and his men with warm hospitality and prepared feasts for them. Their cacique, Agüeybana, paid Ponce an enormous tribute by proposing they exchange names. In a ceremony to cement their bond as brothers, Agüeybana took the name of Ponce de León and Ponce became Agüeybana. In the same ceremony, the cacique's mother took the name of Doña Inez, Ponce's wife.

Leaving his new brother, Agüeybana, Ponce set off to tour the island. On reaching the harbor of San Juan in the north, he reportedly exclaimed, *¡Qué puerto tan rico!* (What a rich port!) For the following decades, the harbor was known as Puerto Rico, while the island continued to be called San Juan Bautista. Eventually, the names were reversed.

For his permanent site, Ponce selected Caparra, a few miles from this harbor, then returned to report his findings to Ovando in Santo Domingo (the capital of Hispaniola). The cacique Agüeybana journeyed to Santo Domingo at the same time. (The distance between the two islands was not great; the Indians of Boriquén often went there in canoes to trade.) Ponce was the perfect host to his guest; he presented him to Governor Ovando.

In 1509, Ponce returned to Puerto Rico with one hundred men. One of them was Juan Garrido, a free black, the first African to step on Puerto Rican soil. Soon thereafter, Ponce was named governor of the island by King Ferdinand, who also ordered him to distribute land and Indians to each of his men and to thirty more colonists being sent from Seville.

In the meantime, Diego Columbus, son of the discoverer, had asserted his hereditary rights to the West Indies and insisted on taking the post of governor of all of them for himself, replacing Ovando. Diego then sent his own man, Juan Ceron, to Puerto Rico to replace Ponce. Thus, it was Ceron who made the initial distribution of Indians to the Spanish colonists. This system, practiced throughout Spanish-controlled islands, was called *repartimientos* or *encomiendas*.

Ceron did not last long. King Ferdinand stepped in and reconfirmed Ponce as governor, with civil and criminal jurisdiction. Ceron was sent back to Spain in chains. Diego Columbus, furious, confiscated Ponce's property in Hispaniola. Their petty rivalries did not alter the fate of the Indians. Under Ponce, the repartimiento system was expanded. Thirty to 300 Indians, with their cacique, were assigned to each colonist. Cacique Agüeybana, Ponce's friend, with all his villagers, was given to a rich nobleman named Don Cristóbal de Sotomayor.

In all but name, the Arawaks became the slaves of the

*Top Left:* Christopher Columbus bids Ferdinand and Isabella of Spain farewell. *Top Right:* Ponce de León. *Bottom:* Slaves were imported to work in the sugar industry.

*Above:* The French pirate Pierre le Grand captures the Vice-Admiral of the Spanish Flotilla. *Below:* The ancient fortress *El Morro* still guards the approach to San Juan, Puerto Rico.

*Right:* General Nelson A. Miles.
*Below:* The 25th Company, Alfonso Guard, Spanish Army, Puerto Rico.

Beautiful stretches of beaches, tobacco plantations, and Puerto Rico's famed tropical rain forest offer visitors exciting scenic contrasts.

*ght:* Old San Juan with its narrow streets
d authentic Spanish architecture.
*low:* An aerial view of new San Juan.

*Above:* A quiet street of comfortable homes. *Below:* A fiesta lights up the night.

*Above:* New industries in Puerto Rico include a drug-producing segment. *Below:* Students mingle near University Tower on the Rio Piedras campus of the University of Puerto Rico.

*Top left:* Former Governor of Puerto Rico, Luis Muñoz Marín. *Top right:* A member of the Young Lords. *Bottom left:* Felisa Rincón de Gautier, well-loved former Mayor of San Juan. *Bottom right:* Rafael Hernandez Colon, newly-elected Governor of Puerto Rico.

Spaniards. Each of them was assigned a certain work quota—in the gold mines, building houses, farms, or other tasks. Those who failed to meet their quotas were severely punished. They were fed poorly, if at all; treated, at best, with indifference but just as often with sadistic brutality; whipped if they tried to escape; slaughtered if they defied their new masters. Men, women, and children were all expected to work from dawn to nightfall without respite. In a very short time, they were dying in alarming numbers.

At Caparra, the site he had selected for his capital, Ponce de León used Indian labor to construct his residence. It was strongly built of stone and brick, decorated with handsome tiles from Seville, and—the only substantial building around—served also as a fortress, as the seat of government, and as a storehouse for arms and important documents. (Only the foundations of this first Spanish edifice on Puerto Rican soil have survived.) Ponce's wife and children joined him at Caparra.

Confident that Puerto Rico had vast gold reserves, Ponce got authorization from the Crown to smelt the gold his Indians mined rather than to ship it to Hispaniola for smelting. Puerto Rico's first gold foundry opened in Caparra in October 1510. Very soon, Ponce sent gold to King Ferdinand worth more than 4000 pesos. This was the "Crown's fifth," which all conquistadors were obliged to turn over to their king. The remaining four-fifths they kept for themselves. The Indians who had mined the gold received only blows to spur them on to greater efforts. Ponce, in a short time, became very rich.

In 1511, Ferdinand showed his formal recognition of the island and, perhaps, his pleasure with the gold by granting San Juan a coat of arms. The coat of arms had a lamb, the symbol of St. John, to signify peace and brotherhood. It bore the letters "F" and "Y" for Ferdinand and his wife Isabella (then spelled Ysabel), and for their personal emblems: *flechas* (arrows) and *yugo* (yoke). In the border design, lions and castles represented Isabella's hereditary kingdoms of León and Castille; flags were those of other kingdoms under her and Ferdinand's rule; crosses, such as were carried by the Crusaders, marked the victory of the royal couple in driving the Moors from Spain. Excluded from the coat of arms, as though unworthy, were any symbols for the New World territories. The coat of arms, almost unchanged, is now the seal of modern Puerto Rico.

# 5 THE INDIANS FIGHT BACK

*"They bear no arms, and are all unprotected and so very cowardly that a thousand would not face three; so they are fit to be ordered about and made to work, to sow and do aught else that may be needed, and you may build towns and teach them to go clothed and to adopt our customs."*

*—Columbus, writing to King Ferdinand*

That the Arawaks of Boriquén did not at once rebel against their Spanish oppressors was not due to cowardice, but to a fatalistic feeling that it would be useless. They had the conviction, encouraged certainly by the Spaniards, that the invaders were immortal. As their plight grew more and more desperate, an old cacique named Urayoán, who lived on the west coast, decided to find out if it was really true that Spaniards never died.

In November 1510, the Spanish colonist, Diego Salcedo, ordered Urayoán to supply Indians to carry him and his baggage across the river Guaorabo. Urayoán gave secret instructions to the men he assigned for this task. When they reached the deepest part of the river, they let Diego Salcedo fall into the water, and held him under for several hours. Afterward, they laid him gently on the river bank and asked his pardon for what they had done, in case he should revive as they half-expected. For another day, they watched him closely. By then, there was no doubt that he was really dead.

Word that the Spaniards were not immortal spread rapidly throughout the island and caused great rejoicing. For the first time since the cruel repartimiento systems had enslaved them, they saw hope of regaining their freedom. But they reckoned without taking into account the superior weaponry and military experience of the Spaniards as well as their clever psychological tactics.

Soon afterward, some Indians in another part of the island seized the Spaniard, Diego Suarez, and brought him to their cacique, Aymamon. An Indian child reported the kidnapping to his master, Captain Diego de Salazar. Salazar rushed to the Indian camp, found Suarez tied to a tree while the Indians were playing pelota. He quickly released him and gave him a sword. Both men held back the Indians, now alerted. Aymamon was wounded, but the Spaniards and the Indian child were untouched. Later, Aymamon praised Salazar for his bravery in fighting against great odds and asked to be allowed to use his name, which he believed must have magical powers.

Don Cristóbal de Sotomayor, who held Ponce's friend, Agüeybana, and his people, was notoriously cruel to his Indians. When Agüeybana died, his nephew, now Agüeybana II, called together all the leading caciques on the island and proposed they unite. They resolved to fight to their death rather than continue a life of blows and humiliations. Sotomayor's interpreter, Juan González was at the meeting and warned his master that an attack was imminent. Hastily, Sotomayor packed his goods, quit his hacienda with his relatives and Spanish servants, and started out for town. En route, Agüeybana led an attack against them. Sotomayor and all his party were killed except for the interpreter, Juan Gonzales, who escaped by promising to be the cacique's slave.

Governor Ponce de León resolved to meet the Indians on their own ground. Leaving the defense of Caparra to Captain Salazar, he set out to Sotomayor's hacienda with a force of 120 men. When they reached Agüeybana's village, they found the Indians having a victory celebration. Ponce's men encircled the village, waited for nightfall when the Indians had fallen asleep, then rushed in with swords and lances, killing many, taking others prisoner.

Agüeybana II rallied his forces later and prepared to attack

Ponce's camp. Forewarned, the Spaniards made a parapet of logs, stones, and earth to stop Indian arrows and brought an arquebus, a portable gun, into position. When the Indians rushed the parapet, the gunner fired down on them. They retreated, leaving their dead and carrying their wounded, but attacked again and again only to suffer more losses. Their last attack was led by Agüeybana II, wearing the golden disc that marked him as a cacique. The gunner fired at him point-blank and killed him on the spot. His warriors fled in disorder.

Governor Ponce, confident that, with the death of Agüeybana, the Indian resistance would end, sent word to all the caciques proposing a truce. Only two agreed; one of these was later baptized and given the Christian name of Alonso. The others continued their attacks—mostly on isolated haciendas—from their hiding places in the mountains of Luquillo and then from nearby islands where they were joined by their former enemies, the Caribs. Governor Ponce, seeing his gold mines bereft of workers, sent out ships to force them back. His men killed more than they were able to capture. Many Indians committed suicide rather than return to work for the Spaniards.

Wanderlust struck the governor in 1513. From the Indians, Ponce de León learned of an exceedingly rich island called Bimini, somewhere north of Cuba. He organized an expedition of several ships and set out to find it. The island turned out to be Florida. Although Ponce found neither gold nor a Fountain of Youth, he had made a momentous discovery. By 1515, he was back in Puerto Rico.

In his absence, the Borinqueños, with their Carib allies, attacked Caparra, where Ponce had his residence, killed some of the inhabitants and destroyed the church and many of the flimsier houses. From Hispaniola, Diego Columbus had sent an expedition to Puerto Rico; they had captured some of the caciques, put them in chains, and sent them back to Diego in Santo Domingo. The Indian rebellion within the island was almost over by the time Ponce returned, but the attacks of the

Caribs on Puerto Rican shores would continue sporadically through the sixteenth century. Up until 1521, Ponce spent much of his time sending unsuccessful expeditions after them.

Over his wishes, the capital of Puerto Rico was moved from Caparra to the present-day island of Old San Juan on the grounds that Caparra was in marshy, unhealthy country and that the road from there to San Juan harbor where the Spanish ships anchored was "infernal." Ponce never lived in San Juan. In 1521, when Puerto Rican gold supplies were already rapidly diminishing, he took off a second time for Florida. King Ferdinand had granted him the title of Governor of Florida and Bimini in addition to his other titles: Captain by Sea and Land of the Island of San Juan Bautista; Lifelong Alderman of the Municipal Council of the City of Puerto Rico; lifelong Captain of the Regiment of Boriquén. These honors did not help when he and his men landed in Florida only to be attacked by the local inhabitants. Ponce de León was mortally wounded by an arrow. The survivors brought their ship to Cuba, where Ponce soon died.

Among the Catholic missionaries who came to the New World at the same time as the conquistadors, there were some protests against the enslavement of the Indians. In 1512, the Dominicans sent Brother Antonio de Montesino to Spain to report their plight to King Ferdinand. As a result, this devoutly Catholic king called a meeting of jurists and theologians to draw up a code of obligations for Spanish colonists: the work hours of the Indians were henceforth to be reduced; no married women or children were to be forced to do heavy work in the mines; all Indians must be baptized and taught to write and read. Before these instructions reached Puerto Rico, the island Indians were already in revolt.

Two years later, King Ferdinand granted permission for the colonists to marry Indian women. It was against Spanish policy to allow Spanish women to go to the islands. Many Spaniards had already helped themselves to Indian "wives." Ferdinand's decree simply made this legitimate. To their favor, the Spaniards, cruel as they were to the Indians, never considered themselves their superiors simply because of their race.

The most ardent defender of the Indians was Father Bartolomé de las Casas, also a Dominican, who came to Santo Domingo in 1502 and was ordained a priest in Puerto Rico in 1512. Indians were assigned to him as to all Spaniards, but he set them free. He pleaded their cause most ardently with King Ferdinand and, after Ferdinand's death in 1516, with the regent, Cardinal Francisco Jiménez de Cisneros, who served as Spain's ruler until Ferdinand's grandson, Charles, came of age.

Father Las Casas' *Historia de Las Indias,* which contained valuable historical and anthropological information about the Indians and also described in graphic detail the atrocities committed against them in all Spanish territories, was begun in 1527 and not published until 1875. But as a result of his efforts, some humanitarian laws to protect the Indians were enacted in 1542; it was already too late.

No one knows exactly how many Indians were in Puerto Rico when Columbus landed. They were "as thick as bees," according to Father Las Casas; 40,000 is considered a moderate estimate. The population shrank with incredible rapidity from overwork, starvation, torture, murder, and massacres in battle, in addition to a dreadful smallpox epidemic supposedly brought in with the African slaves. By a 1514 census, the Indian population was estimated at 4000. In 1530, the year when it was admitted that the gold mines were exhausted, another census reported only 1148 Indians left. By 1582, less than a century after Columbus discovered Puerto Rico, the Spanish government announced that not a single Indian remained alive on the island.

This was, perhaps, an exaggeration. An uncounted number of Indians escaped the Spanish by hiding in the mountains. In remote villages, there are people with the physical traits of pure-blooded Arawaks. Some Indians later married escaped black slaves or poor white farmers; their descendants have the high cheekbones and straight, black silky hair of the Indians. That many descendants of the original Spanish colonists also have Indian blood is beyond doubt.

The Indian influence has survived in other ways. Indian music and folklore, combined with that of Africa brought over with the slaves, has provided a rich cultural legacy among the farmer peasants and mountain people. Towns named for Indian caciques dot the island: Utuado, Yabucoa, Gurabo, Cayey, Guainabo. Indian words became part of the Spanish vocabulary and were later adapted in English: hammock, canoe, tobacco, key (for a reef or low island), maize (the Indian name for corn). But the gentle Arawaks of Boriquén will never again assemble in their batey before the house of their cacique, to feast, or play games, or give pageant-operas. Their lives, their way of life, were sacrificed to the greed of the strangers they trusted.

# 6 THE MAKING OF A SPANISH COLONY

"Here lies the very illustrious Señor Juan Ponce de León, first governor of Florida, first conquistador and governor of this island of San Juan."
— Inscription on his marble sepulcher

While Ponce de León was away on his last and fatal visit to Florida, his son-in-law, Garcia Troche, husband of his oldest daughter Juana, built a new house for him in Old San Juan, a house he would never see. Called the *Casa Blanca* (the White House), it was destroyed by a hurricane in 1523 and rebuilt more sturdily of stone and cement. Ponce's descendants lived in it for more than 250 years.

His family brought Ponce's remains back from Cuba and had them placed in a sepulcher in the San José Church in Cristo Street, San Juan. Much later, across the street from the church in San José Plaza, a statue of him was erected, built of cannon captured from the British in 1797. One of the longest streets in modern San Juan is Avenue Ponce de León. The city of Ponce was named after him. In the minds of Puerto Ricans, he ranks with Columbus as a folklore hero. Of the 150 Spanish governors who ruled Puerto Rico up until 1898, some fairly decent, some very bad, almost all are forgotten except for Ponce de León.

By 1530, less than a decade after Ponce's death, San Juan had a total of 120 stone houses in addition to others of timber with thatched roofs. Only the Casa Blanca was fortified enough to fire on the Caribs when they entered the harbor on their periodic raids, but their shells went notably far from the mark. Terrified women in the settlement with their children took refuge in beautiful Dominican Convent (now the Institute of Culture), which was begun in 1523 and had its cells completed by 1529. Appeals to Spain for a strong fort were, as yet, ignored.

It was a bad year for the small band of colonists, the beginning of a period of hard times. With the gold supply exhausted, they had turned to agriculture, but the new sugar plantations were not yet productive. Three hurricanes struck in succession in 1530, doing enormous damage. There were hardly any Indians left to do the drudgery. Spanish *hidalgos* (sons of somebody) were too much the fine gentlemen to do hard physical work. They bought black slaves but had to borrow money to pay for them. Some fell so deeply in debt that they fled to the mountains so as not to be thrown in debtors' prison. Some committed suicide to avoid public disgrace. One might say they were being justly punished for their hideous treatment of the Indians.

In the midst of their misery, news came of Hernando Cortez' triumph over Montezuma's Aztecs in Mexico and Francisco Pizarro's subsequent conquest of the Incas in Peru. The fabulous treasures of these two kingdoms, now in the hands of the Spaniards, far outshone anything found in the West Indies. The Puerto Rican colonists were utterly dazzled. So many of them decided to leave their unprofitable island to try their luck on the continent that the governor forbid further departures on the penalty of death. When the exodus continued, he tried to stop it by encouraging agriculture, especially more sugar plantations and ginger. He built water mills, imported coconut palms, guinea hens, cattle, and horses.

In Spain, Puerto Rico suddenly acquired new importance as a waylay station where ships bearing precious cargo from Mexico and Peru could refuel and stop for water. Belated recognition was made that this might be dangerous for the Puerto Ricans. In 1533, King Charles I of Spain (who also had the title of Charles V, Emperor of the Holy Roman Empire), grandson of Ferdinand and Isabella, authorized Puerto Rico's first fort on the western shore of the little island of San Juan. Seven years later, when it was considered complete, it consisted merely of a circular tower, an underground dungeon, and four walls enclosing a patio. Moreover, it was built so far from the entrance to San Juan harbor that one contemporary historian commented, "Even blind men could not have chosen a more inappropriate site."

This was La Fortaleza, which would be remodeled; enlarged; turned into a palace with marble floors, tiled stairways, high ceilings, shuttered doors opening on long galleries; enhanced by a surrounding garden filled with rare and precious trees and flowering shrubs; and used as the governor's residence.

In 1556, King Charles I abdicated the throne of Spain in favor of his son, Philip II, and retired to a monastery. At this period and for the next three decades, Spain was at the height of her glory. Her vast world empire was unrivaled. Spanish literature and art flourished. Wealth poured in from the New World—to be spent recklessly, mostly on war. The common people of Spain did not profit an iota. The first signal of Spanish decline, which continued at a headlong pace, was in 1588 when Britain defeated the Spanish Armada.

Throughout all this, Puerto Rico remained a stepchild. It was not uncommon for a year or more to lapse between visits of Spanish cargo ships. Thus, Puerto Ricans had no way to ship sugar, ginger, and leather to Spain. By royal decree, they were forbidden to trade directly with other nations or other Caribbean islands. Their economy suffered drastically. A bishop, who arrived in 1572, reported the island was so poor that neither candles nor oil for his church lamps could be found.

Yet, with all its hardships and handicaps, the Spanish colony of Puerto Rico was growing, putting down roots, becoming entrenched. By 1600, San Juan had become a Spanish town with the charm of towns in the homeland.

Besides San José Church, it now had a great cathedral, the Cathedral of San Juan Bautista, where Ponce's sepulcher would be transferred—with a circular stairway, vaulted Gothic ceilings, and an excellent organ brought over from Spain. An English observer commented that it was "perhaps more perfect and handsomer" than any English cathedral. The same observer waxed enthusiastic about El Convento, the Dominican Convent which had harbored women and children refugees from the Caribs, both for its appearance and its superb view over the bay.

The private homes, he noted, were Spanish style, "with two stories only, but very solid . . . the rooms are large and pleasant, and with large doors in place of windows to let in plenty of air." By now, about 170 families were prosperous enough to live in such palatial houses. Most of them had brick terraces, pleasant gardens, and high, stone walls around them. In the outskirts were still primitive huts for the less fortunate. There were no natural springs; the water supply depended on rain collected in reservoirs. Two hospitals had been built. On orders from the Spanish Crown, children received some schooling from the Franciscan friars. The rest of the island had only a few hamlets—San Germán was the largest. Some rich colonists had haciendas on the coastal plains where they raised sugar cane with the aid of slave labor.

A class society had grown up. Leading colonists had their individual coats of arms, granted by the Crown for "distinguished service in conquest." The descendants of Ponce de León were the aristocracy. They enhanced their social position by marriages in the families of governors, royal officials, and bishops. Spaniards born in Spain were rated higher socially than those born in Puerto Rico, who were called Creoles. Children of mixed marriages were not discriminated against, except that they were not permitted to hold government positions. Creoles rarely were given such positions either. A white lower class had been created by the export from Spain of convicts and others whom the Spanish government considered undesirable.

One thing can be said about these Spanish settlers. They were colonists in the true meaning of the word. Adventure and lure of gold may have brought them to Puerto Rico, but unlike many colonists of other European powers, especially the French, the Belgians, and the English, they thought of the New World not the Old World as their permanent home. With the conviction that they and their families would always live there, they set about making Puerto Rico into a little Spain, in architecture and in customs.

Like towns in Spain, each Puerto Rican town had its patron saint. Hand-carved and painted *santos* (saints) became the island's most valued folk art. On its saint's day, each town held a religious fiesta. There was singing and dancing in the streets. People paraded in bizarre costumes and masks. Prizes were given. The governor and royal officials, seated on horses adorned with velvet trimmed in gold or silver, acted as the judges. Country people from miles around walked to town to join in the colorful celebrations. Although Spanish rule ceased nearly three-quarters of a century ago and Puerto Rico is no longer totally Catholic, the saint's day festivals are still held in town after town every month of the year.

# 7 THE AFRICAN SLAVES

*"We do not seek reforms for the whites if they will not liberate the blacks."*
— Segundo Ruiz Belvis, Nineteenth-century
Puerto Rican abolitionist

Contrary to what people said later, the Spanish did not wait until after the Indians had disappeared before they started bringing black slaves to the West Indies. The Spanish Crown first authorized their importation in 1501, with the restriction they must come from Spain, not directly from Africa. Africans had been brought to Spain as slaves by the Moors several centuries before. The government reasoned that their descendants would be Christians and could thus serve as moral examples to the "heathen" Indians. Instead, the first blacks, mostly household servants, quickly allied themselves with the Indians on the ground that both black and brown were unjustly deprived of their liberty.

Governor of the West Indies Nicolás de Ovando, in alarm, begged Spain to stop sending black servants. The suspension, put in effect, lasted only a year. In 1504, after Queen Isabella's death, King Ferdinand lifted the ban.

In 1505, Vicente Yañez Pinzón, the first, and absentee governor of Puerto Rico, received authorization to import Africans from Africa as slaves, but nothing was done about it. Diego Columbus and his officials are known to have purchased one hundred West Coast Africans from the Portuguese in 1510. Two years later, Ponce de León, then governor of Puerto Rico, was granted permission to admit three male and three female Christian slaves to serve his son, Don Luis.

When Father Bartolomé Las Casas was in Spain, pleading the cause of the oppressed Indians, he once suggested that Africans be imported to work in the mines and do other tasks obviously too hard for the slight Indians. Later his conscience troubled him deeply, though in truth whatever he said or did not say would have made no difference. The conquistadors and the royal officials in the West Indies considered menial work far beneath them. With the Indians gone, it was inevitable for them to seek another source of supply.

In 1518, King Charles I licensed a Flemish nobleman to bring 4000 African slaves to sell in the Antilles. This was one of a series of royal licenses granted to court favorites and marked the opening of the West African slave trade as a mass industry. The license-holders turned first to Portugal, which had led Europe in exploring the West Coast of Africa and was the first to discover that the black natives were profitable merchandise. Later, other European nations, including Spain, as well as the United States entered this lucrative business. More accurately, private companies or shipowners became slave traders with the support of their home governments.

The human cargo was transported from African shores to the New World in such unspeakable conditions that they died in great numbers. On occasion, whole shiploads perished of scurvy or yellow fever. The slavers never seemed to learn that treating their captives humanely would be to their own advantage. The Portuguese, it is said, simply sprinkled the prisoners with holy water and entrusted them to God.

Africans who survived the filth, disease, and revolting diet of the slave ships had to be of remarkably strong constitution. Some Spanish colonists boasted you could not kill a Negro except by hanging, which was, of course, nonsense. Blacks died of overwork and mistreatment as the Indians had, with the difference that, when Indians were gone, there were no more. Africa seemed to have an inexhaustible source of slave labor. Cuba paid three hundred dollars a head and accepted only males, buying more when needed. Puerto Rico, comparatively poor, bought an equal number of male and female slaves, so that they would mate and produce future slaves. It was all quite calculated and cold-blooded.

The first rebellion of African slaves was in Hispaniola in 1522. Five years later, there was a similar uprising in Puerto Rico. In both islands, Africans joined Indians to form guerrilla bands, but the revolts were put down as the purely Indian ones had been. During the more than three and a half centuries that slavery continued in Puerto Rico, it was not uncommon for slaves to flee from their masters and hide out in the mountains where they could live off the land on native fruits and roots with less labor and better than in captivity. But after that first uprising, there were no general slave rebellions such as those in Haiti, Martinique, and St. Croix in the Virgin Islands.

When it was evident that the Africans could not get gold out of the exhausted gold mines, they were employed elsewhere. In 1539, they were set to work on a new fort designed to replace the inadequate La Fortaleza. This was El Morro (*morro* means promontory), on the triangular promontory in the northwest corner of Old San Juan, between the bay and the Atlantic. It was an excellent location for protection of the new community, but work proceeded with exasperating slowness. It was said without exaggeration that Negro youths turned into old men on this job.

From the seventeenth century on, the major use for African slave labor was on sugar plantations. By the early 1800's, there were hundreds of small sugar haciendas along the length of Puerto Rico's southern coast, mostly owned by single families. In addition to black slaves, the owners employed poor whites. Their lot was little better than the blacks. An edict of 1849 literally transformed these whites into a forced labor group. After 1849, poor whites could not travel without passes and they could not leave their jobs without permission.

Side by side, blacks and whites dug irrigation ditches, bent over hours on end to plant the cane stalk cuttings, cut the cane with their machetes at an "awesome and painful" pace, loaded the cane on ox wagons for transport. The hot sun burned them. The thick mud impeded their steps. Fine dust from the cane lodged in their skin and nostrils. Insects were a constant annoyance. The *mayordomo* (foreman) astride his mare and whip in hand, kept constant watch for laggards and slackers.

Salvador Brau, eighteenth-century Puerto Rican historian and humanitarian, referred to the island as a place where "national well being was based on the national shame of slave labor," and where "rhythms of the zamba and the crack of the driving whip joined together in a single echo." His words could have applied with equal truth all over the West Indies and to all the slaveholding nations. Puerto Rico was neither the best nor the worst.

Yet, there were some compensations for the slaves and forced laborers on Puerto Rican sugar plantations. In spite of the whips of their foremen, the hacienda owners, indolent men and not too ambitious, often took a paternal role toward their workers, provided that they acted sufficiently grateful and docile. Each family might be granted a plot of land to grow his own vegetables; permitted to collect firewood or graze a few beasts on hacienda land; and use the hacienda grindstone to grind cornmeal. Some *patrons* kept a cane field apart to provide the aged and infirm with sugar and, perhaps, rum at Christmas. In return, the "grateful" slaves might serenade the patron and his family or name their children after him. It did no harm, whatever their secret thoughts, and made life easier for them.

There were a few other advantages to being a slave in a Spanish Catholic-dominated colony. A few Catholic fathers of the same genre as Bartolomé de las Casas tried to relieve their misery, especially during their terrible and terrifying first days. The Spaniards sometimes allowed their slaves to work for themselves on Sundays and religious feast days and thus earn money to buy their freedom. In 1848, the Crown ruled that children of slaves could be granted freedom at the time of their baptism, on a payment of a mere twenty-five pesos for each one.

Puerto Rico eventually became a haven for runaway slaves from neighboring islands. Spanish authorities welcomed them and allowed them to stay as free men, if they accepted the Catholic religion and swore loyalty to the Spanish Crown. Freed slaves met little discrimination because of their color, except for the ruling that civil officials and military officers must be pure-blooded Spaniards, a law not revoked until 1870. Marriages between whites and blacks were perfectly legal, as marriages with Indians had been. Many blacks and mulattoes have risen to high political and professional posts in Puerto Rico.

Not even full equality can erase the scars of their long and cruel bondage. Who can forget the barbarous practice of the authorities of branding on the forehead with a hot iron all slaves brought into the island legally? The official excuse was that many slaves were brought in at cut-rate prices by English slave traders or were kidnapped from other islands by unscrupulous sea captains for resale in Puerto Rico. Periodically, all unbranded slaves were rounded up—as though they were the criminals—then branded and sold at public auction.

Or who could forget Governor General Juan Prim's *Bando Contra La Raza Africana* (Ban Against the African Race) of 1849, the harshest penal code ever directed against slaves in Spanish history? The official excuse for this piece of legislation was that it was needed to keep slaves from rebelling as they were doing right and left elsewhere. The irony was that the slave trade was already illegal; the British, who had freed their slaves in 1836, were patrolling West African coasts to prevent illicit slave smuggling.

The abolition movement, which had started in England, spread to other European countries and to the United States. People of good will everywhere recognized that it was morally wrong to enslave other human beings. In Puerto Rico, emancipation of slaves was proceeding at a gradual pace during the Civil War in America. On March 22, 1873, abolition of all slaves was formally declared. In Ponce, the triangular *Parque de la Abolicion* (Abolition Park) is the scene of an annual festival celebrating the date of liberation.

Africans never outnumbered Europeans in Puerto Rico as they did on many Caribbean islands. A census in 1765 gave a total of 44,883 population, of which 5037 were slaves—in contrast to the Danish colony of St. Croix in the Virgin Islands where 30,000 black slaves served 300 whites. By 1860, of Puerto Rico's total population of 583,181, there were 41,736 slaves. The proportion decreased rapidly from then on.

The percentage of blacks to whites in Puerto Rico is estimated today at about the same as in mainland United States. There is one great difference. In the United States, it has been customary to penalize any person with even a trace of black blood. Nothing of the sort exists in Puerto Rico. A race-conscious American, commenting on the absence of blacks in a large government office, was silenced by the comment of her Puerto Rican host: "Madame, there is no one here without some black blood."

# 8 CORSAIRS, BUCCANEERS, AND SMUGGLERS

*"Whoever has viewed the fortifications of Puerto Rico must feel surprised that, In the year 1797, the English under Ralph Abercromby, with a force of scarcely 10,000 men, should lay siege to this place...."*
— Colonel George Flinter,
Irish military analyst

San Juan's first forts, La Fortaleza and El Morro, were originally conceived as protection against the Indians, especially the Caribs. Even before the Arawaks and the Caribs ceased to be a threat, the Spaniards had come to realize that their most dangerous enemies were their fellow Europeans.

By an edict of the Pope, the "non-Christian world" was to be divided between Portugal, who had occupied Brazil, and Spain. The rest of Europe, duly piqued, refused to comply. When the Spanish ambassador quoted the Pope to Francis I, King of France, the latter retorted: "Show me Father Adam's testament by which he divided the world between my brothers of Spain and Portugal." As the Spanish ambassador was unable to produce a will from Adam or Eve, the French went on considering they had as much right to the treasures of the New World as anyone else.

As early as 1528, they landed at San Germán and burned its still-primitive thatched houses. A French armada of three ships again raided San Germán in 1543. Most of the remaining inhabitants then moved inland and established New San Germán. The French, for some reason, attacked and destroyed the near-abandoned site the next year.

These early raids were a prelude of a gigantic squabble over the islands, and treasures, and kingdoms that Spain had so confidently expected to keep for herself. On into the seventeenth and eighteenth centuries, European ships of other nations roamed the seas; seized Spanish cargo ships; attacked and, sometimes, occupied Spanish settlements. These pirates—for that was what they were—were known by the more polite words of buccaneers or corsairs. They had the blessing of their home governments and sometimes acted under their countries' orders.

The Spanish, who had been equally lawless toward the people of the lands they had occupied, set about with great self-righteousness to build up their defenses. In 1589, two celebrated military architects, Juan Bautista Antonelli and Juan de Tejada, were sent from Spain to redesign and finish El Morro, which had been under construction for 50 years. Antonelli's plan involved laying a "hornwork"—great walls up to 40 feet thick in the shape of a bull's-horn lying across the promontory—to give protection against both land and sea attacks.

Among the 400 laborers put to work to build these walls were black slaves who had been on the project back in 1539. There were also Creoles and Chinese coolies imported from China. The walls were finished in 4 years. The Chinese were sent home, but it is said they never again saw China; their captain, to save time and trouble, dumped them out once he was on the high seas.

The El Morro hornwork was barely completed when, in 1595, a Spanish fleet, carrying some thirty-five tons of gold and silver from the mainland, stopped in San Juan harbor for repairs. During the 7 months it took for the repairs, the gold and silver was transferred for safety to the tower room of La Fortaleza.

Word of this immense treasure reached the famed, red-bearded Sir Francis Drake, who had a commission as a privateer from Queen Elizabeth of England. He anchored his fleet at the opposite end of Old San Juan from El Morro, near the Puerto Rican mainland, and prepared to land. Unknown to him, the lagoon there was protected by the small Fort Boqueron, which opened fire. One shot pierced the captain's cabin and mortally wounded several officers. The rumor was that one of these was

Drake's second in command, the notorious slave trader and pirate, Sir John Hawkins, who died soon afterward.

Drake withdrew after this setback to the border of San Juan harbor near tiny Cabras (Goat Island). Governor Pedro Suarez promptly summoned all available manpower, including the crews of the treasure ships, and ordered that several Spanish ships be anchored at the entrance of the bay. At night, Sir Francis sent out twenty-five launches with fifty men each to set fire to the Spanish ships. Two of them blazed so brilliantly they lit up the entire harbor and made perfect targets of the British boats. The El Morro gunners sank many of them; several hundred British seamen were lost.

The disaster blighted Sir Francis Drake's career; a year later, he died aboard his own ship. While the Puerto Ricans were celebrating their escape from falling into the clutches of the "terrible English," Queen Elizabeth in England plotted her revenge. To her new favorite, Sir George Clifford, the Earl of Cumberland, she granted a fleet of twenty ships and 4000 men, far more than Drake had commanded. Cumberland's flagship, *Scourge of Malice*, was the most powerful man-o'-war on the seas. He sailed early in 1598 with instructions to take over Puerto Rico for his queen.

In June, Cumberland landed on the deserted beach of Boca de Cangrejos (now Santurce in modern San Juan) and started a land march toward Old San Juan. They failed to get there, in part, because of the fire from Fort Boqueron and, in part, because of the heroic defense of the bridge across the narrow canal between San Juan and the mainland. Two handsome Puerto Rican brothers, Juan and Simón Sanabrias, gave their lives in that defense. Ever since, the bridge has been called *El Puente de Dos Hermanos* (the Bridge of the Two Brothers).

The English finally tried to wade the canal, but nearly drowned because of the weight of their armor. Cumberland then withdrew and ordered another landing—directly on San Juan Island almost midway between Fort Boqueron and El Morro. This time, they were successful and marched into the town unopposed.

The governor, Don Antonio de Mosquero, took refuge with the soldiers at El Morro. Most of the leading citizens fled to the mountains. Cumberland occupied La Fortaleza, and his men bombarded El Morro until they surrendered. His fleet sailed triumphantly into San Juan harbor. Cumberland formally took possession of Puerto Rico, in the name of his sovereign, Queen Elizabeth. Puerto Rico seemed fated to become a British colony.

They were saved by an epidemic of dysentery which spread rapidly among the British invaders, killing many of them and completely demoralizing the troops. Cumberland left with part of his weakened forces on August 24. They took along the San Juan cannons, as well as the bells, religious relics, works of art, and the magnificent organ from the Cathedral San Juan Bautista. Cumberland's second in command Sir John Berkeley stayed on another month with the rest of the troops but left after pillaging the town and loading their ships with hides, ginger, and sugar.

All their plunder did not appease Queen Elizabeth, who noted that it was not worth half the cost of the expedition and could not make up for the loss of some 600 men, mainly through disease.

In Puerto Rico, after the wildest of celebrations, people set out to rebuild their ravaged city and to repair the damaged ramparts of El Morro. Work was begun on an even more massive fort, San Cristóbal, on a promontory facing the Atlantic Ocean—about half a mile east of El Morro—which, if it had been built before, could have prevented Cumberland's easy landing.

San Juan's growing reputation as impregnable did not deter an attack from the Dutch in 1625. On September 25, a powerful fleet with seventeen ships, of the Dutch West India Company, under Captain Boudewijn Hendrikszoon, anchored off San Juan harbor. They stayed there for several weeks, holding San Juan in a state of siege.

Repeatedly, the Dutch captain demanded that El Morro surrender, but there was no answer. He finally sent an ultimatum to Governor Juan de Haro: "Surrender El Morro or we burn the town." The governor sent his reply: "The settlers have enough courage to rebuild their homes, for there is timber in the mountains and building materials on the land."

The Dutch bombarded and occupied San Juan and set fire to La Fortaleza and other buildings, but the Puerto Ricans fought them off with such ferocity that Captain Hendrikszoon raised his siege and left.

Once more, the Puerto Ricans rebuilt their capital and increased their defenses. They started a wall around San Juan 50 feet high in places; it was another century before it was completed. In 1765, two Spaniards with Irish names, Field Marshall Alejandro O'Reilly and Engineer Tomás (Thomas) O'Daly, came from Spain to supervise the fortifications. By 1783, El Morro was completed, as it is today—a single unit with six levels rising 140 feet above the harbor entrance. Fort San Cristóbal was transformed from a mere redoubt to an even more formidable fortification than El Morro. Designed according to the most up to date military structures of the period, it had five independent units—like little forts—connected by tunnels and dry moats to the main structure. The entire San Cristóbal complex covered 27 acres and rose 150 feet above the ocean.

By the last decade of the eighteenth century, San Juan was said to be the most fortified base in the American hemisphere, with the possible exception of Cartagena in Colombia. This reputation did not deter one last attempt on the part of the British to take the island. Lieutenant General Sir Ralph Abercromby reached Puerto Rican shores in 1797, after having taken over defenseless Trinidad "like a ripe plum." He took it for granted that Puerto Rico would fall just as easily.

Like his British predecessors, Abercromby attempted a landing on the mainland, choosing the Boca de Cangrejos (literally, Mouth of Crabs) as Cumberland had done. But Puerto Rico's military governor, Ramon de Castro, had been forewarned and had mobilized the entire country. Some 20,000 jíbaros (mountain farmers) streamed down from the hills to join the soldiers. They were further reinforced by French refugees from Haiti, where black slaves had set up their own government under Toussaint L'Ouverture.

In face of this unexpected resistance, Abercromby withdrew and set sail but tried again to land on the beaches of Condado. Although met with devastating fire, Abercromby held out for another month. On April 30, 1797, he gave up, reporting that "no Act of Vigour on our Part, nor that of any Combined Operation between the Sea and Land service, could in any Manner avail."

Abercromby's withdrawal marked the end of the last serious attempt of any European power to take Puerto Rico by force.

While protecting their island, Puerto Ricans learned some of the aggressive tactics of their attackers. Since regulations of the Crown still forbid them to trade anywhere but with Spain and since Spanish cargo ships still stopped rarely, they would have had no market for their goods had they abided by the law. Instead, they turned to smuggling on a large scale.

Very early in the island's history, they smuggled out goods to neighboring islands. The trade increased mightily on into the seventeenth and eighteenth centuries, after other European powers began to grab West Indies islands away from Spain. Sloops regularly moved into small and inconspicuous harbors on the west, south, and east coasts of Puerto Rico. They were manned by English traders from Jamaica, Danes from the Virgin Islands, French from Martinique, Dutch from Curaçao. They bartered slaves, cloth, tools, and farm implements with the Puerto Ricans in exchange for mules, cattle, hogs, tobacco, fresh fruits, and coffee. There were times when the markets of San Juan were empty of produce, while a few miles away farmers and coastal dwellers were loading foreign vessels with foodstuffs.

Local Puerto Rican authorities, for a price, turned their backs on the traffic. Officers of the Crown, royal officials, soldiers, and even priests and friars took their cut of the profits at one time or another. One governor was found guilty of taking bribes and was removed. His replacement was soon equally involved. The smuggling brought a certain amount of prosperity to the island, but the government in Spain was outraged since they did not profit at all. All their efforts to bring the smugglers to justice proved futile.

By the end of the seventeenth century, the smugglers were turning to piracy and riding the seas in search of ships to plunder. Henry Morgan, the English dean of buccaneers himself, complained indignantly of the "unchristianlike conduct and unneighborliness" of his Puerto Rican rivals.

One of the most successful Puerto Rican pirates was Michael Henríquez, a mulatto and an ex-cobbler, who scouted the Caribbean in search of loot for more than 30 years. The English called him the "Great Arch Villian" and claimed he had more power than the governor, which may have been true.

Another notorious pirate was Robert Cofresí, known as Puerto Rico's Robin Hood, since he robbed from the rich to give to the poor. By his thinking, the rich were the British. He had a special reason for hating them. His father, a smuggler himself, had once rowed out supplies to a British vessel. Instead of paying him, the drunken British officers threw him into the sea. Cofresí vowed to get revenge. Until he was captured by combined Spanish-American-British efforts, he attacked and sank every British ship he could locate.

The mismanagement, corruption, and arbitrary rulings of the Spanish government taught Puerto Ricans that, if they were to survive, they had to use every trick in the book. Continually hard-pressed themselves, they gained a reputation of being hospitable and generous, of being always ready to share what they had with runaway sailors or other unfortunates. They developed a buoyancy, a roistrous sense of humor, and a cynicism toward what is now called the Establishment, that have remained Puerto Rican characteristics to this day.

# 9 CIVIL RIGHTS STRUGGLE

*"I was not born to sing the notes of the nightingale in the city enslaved."*

— Luis Muñoz Rivera

The constant danger from outside enemies did not, as one might think, unite Puerto Ricans of all classes. The aristocracy remained aloof and retained a fantastic snobbery. An early writer noted that when the foppish Castilian Grandee, Duke of Escalona, landed in Puerto Rico, it was "the most splendid event" since the island's discovery. These people dressed with the elegance of the Spanish courts, gave banquets and balls in the style of European royalty, lived in San Juan's finest mansions. Government officials wrote endless memos about whether cockfighting should be made illegal, but displayed no curiosity at all as to how poor people managed to eat. They ignored completely the rich folk culture, with its Indian and African legacy combined with Christian mysticism, rising in the island's interior.

The governors, all appointed by the Spanish Crown, took the attitude that if they provided the people with plenty of fiestas, they would never make trouble. One governor stated that the islanders could be ruled properly "with a whip and a violin." For political reasons, Spain sided against England and with the Americans during the American Revolution. After the Americans were victorious, the Spanish government imposed a strict censorship on their colonies to keep out books and journals which might spread dangerous ideas about freedom and independence. (In 1862, the banned books included Victor Hugo's *Les Miserables*.)

In spite of their censorship, dangerous ideas seaped into a large part of Spanish America. Heroes of liberation movements emerged—José de San Martín and Simon Bolivar in South America, Father Miguel Hidalgo in Mexico. The ferment spread to the West Indies, but Puerto Rico remained calm.

The Spain of the post-American Revolution period, shorn of her overseas territories one after another, continued in a steady decline from the great empire of the days of Cortez and Pizarro. Her crowning humiliation came in 1808 when Napoleon added her to his conquests and set his inefficient brother, Joseph Bonaparte, on the Spanish throne—a post he managed to hold for 5 long years.

The Spanish province of Cadiz became the home of the government-in-exile. In the capital city of Cadiz, the *Cortes* (National Assembly) met and drew up the most liberal constitution the Spanish monarchy had ever known. Puerto Rico, as one of the few loyal territories left, was a principal beneficiary. By decree, the island was pronounced a Spanish province. Its inhabitants, except slaves, would henceforth be Spanish citizens with the right to elect their own deputy to represent them at the Cortes.

The island's first elected deputy was Ramón Power Giralt, a charming and handsome young man, born in San Juan of Spanish parents and educated in Spain. He proved so eloquent and persuasive that, within a year after he arrived in Spain, he was made vice president of the Cortes. All his energies were devoted to improving the lot of his fellow Puerto Ricans. The long list of demands he presented to the Assembly covered tax reforms, land reforms, trade concessions to discourage smuggling, the building of a vocational school, a university, and more hospitals. He also insisted that Puerto Ricans be given preferential rights over the Spanish-born for government jobs.

The university Power Giralt wanted would not be built until 1903. A request for a college of pre-university level was crushed by the governor. Those who wanted to study could go to Spain, he said. As for those who did not have the money to travel, it was all to the good; all the poor needed to know was reading, writing, and Christian doctrine. Attending schools in the United States was also discouraged by the authorities on the grounds that the students would be exposed to non-Catholic thinking.

With these exceptions, Power Giralt's demands were nearly all granted. The Spanish government, chastened by its losses, felt it better to give into this dedicated young man than to lose Puerto Rico altogether. He died of yellow fever in Cadiz in 1813, without knowing how much he had won.

As one result of his efforts, an enlightened Spanish official, Alejandro Ramírez, was sent to Puerto Rico to administer royal funds and promote trade, industry, and agriculture. Free trade with foreign ports was tardily permitted, and an expansive trade with the United States was established. Legitimate export trade jumped from $269,000 in 1813 to $2 million in 1818. Now that coffee, a favorite contraband product, could be sold legitimately, settlers flocked to start coffee plantations in the rocky mountain soil. Coffee exports in the 1890's were triple that of sugar exports, but coffee workers were paid even less than sugarcane workers.

With money pouring in, the rich had more time for a social and cultural life. More homes, churches, and public buildings were constructed of native materials, but in the style of Spain. Gray-blue tiles, known as *adoquines*, brought over in Spanish ships as ballast, paved many of San Juan's picturesque streets. The nineteenth century saw Ponce, Mayagüez, San Germán and other towns rival San Juan in architectural beauty. The theater was introduced from Spain. Art, poetry, and literature were encouraged. Political parties appeared: the conservatives, who were content with Spanish rule but sought even closer ties; and the liberals, who wanted less interference from Spain.

An abortive rebellion took place in 1868, known as the *Grito de Lares* (the Cry of Lares). On September 20 of that year, a band of several hundred persons of all classes from slaveowners to slaves marched into the small mountain town of Lares, and woke up the population, crying "Viva Independence . . . ! Down with Spain . . . ! Death to the Spaniards!" When the mayor protested, they put him into his own jail.

The next day the rebels proclaimed the "Republic of Boriquén" and named a small landholder, Francisco Ramírez, as provisional president. In the mayor's office, the portrait of the Spanish Queen was replaced with the inscription: "Long Live Free Puerto Rico! Liberty or Death! 1868." In their manifesto, the rebels proclaimed that as of that date all children born of slave mothers should be free. Their major grievance was the pass system, which imposed forced labor on free men.

The rebellion did not last. Many of the demonstrators returned to their homes in the next few days. Some of their leaders were seized and thrown into jail. But, in time, the Grito de Lares became a symbol of freedom in the minds of Puerto Ricans, much like the Boston Massacre in America, far exceeding what it actually was.

Among the progressive and educated elite in Ponce during this period, the talk was not of independence but of reform. One of this group was Ramón Baldorioty de Castro, who returned from his university studies in Madrid to form the Liberal Party of Ponce. Another was Ramón Marín, a playwright, an abolitionist, a private school principal, and editor of the political journal, *La Crónica*. When the wealthy parents of his students paid Ramón Marín in slaves, he promptly set them free.

They were joined by an ardent young man from Barranquitas in the mountains named Luis Muñoz Rivera. His father had wanted him to go into his business, but he had decided to make poetry his life's work. Ramón Marín had published several of his poems, which were very good, in *La Crónica*. Muñoz Rivera came to Ponce to meet his editor and at once was caught up in the fervor of his ideals and joined the Liberal Party. In 1887, a few years later, with Baldorioty and Ramón Marín, Muñoz founded the *Partido Autonomista* (the Autonomist Party), which openly advocated self-government and a dominion status in relation to Spain.

The Autonomist Party's activities were suppressed by Governor Romuldo Palacio, who considered their platform treason. Under his reign of terror, military law was declared; Baldorioty and Ramón Marín were incarcerated in El Morro; and the charming poet-patriot, Lola Rodríguez de Tió, another active party member, was exiled. Soldiers traveled across the island, arresting and torturing suspects. Like many dictators, the governor's attempts at suppression only strengthened the opposition. Protests to Spain from liberal Puerto Ricans brought about his recall.

In 1891, Luis Muñoz Rivera began publishing the newspaper, *La Democracia,* which exposed Spain's injustice toward the island colony and advocated not independence but a maximum of self-rule. To promote this cause, Muñoz Rivera went to Spain in 1897, as one of a three-man commission. The conservative leaders then in power evaded him, but he had a long talk with the leader of the Spanish Liberal Party, Práxedes Mateo Sagasta, who made out a list of things he would do for Puerto Rico if his party came to power. It did so that November. Mateo Sagasta kept his word and granted Puerto Rico a Charter of Autonomy.

The charter gave Puerto Rico the status of a dominion—as the Autonomist Party had wanted—and more self-government than they had ever had. Henceforth, Puerto Rico would have full freedom in external trade, thus settling an old grievance. It would have a parliament with two houses, one elected by the people, the other partly elected and partly appointed. All parliament members had to have property yielding at least 4000 pesos annually. There were, likewise, severe restrictions on who could vote. The governor, still an appointee of the Spanish Crown and representative of the interests of Spain, still had the final say. Under the charter, Luis Muñoz Rivera became Puerto Rico's first prime minister.

In less than a year in office, he eliminated Crown taxes, stamp taxes, license taxes, taxes on fish, and fees for judicial action, thus reducing Puerto Rico's tax burden by about 1.5 million dollars. It is still a matter of speculation as to how much more might have been achieved for Puerto Rico under the charter, if their ties with Spain had not been abruptly severed.

By 1898, Puerto Rico had a population of about one million. There were 35,000 people in San Juan. Eighteen other towns had a population of more than 2500. Spain had built a military road across the mountains—from north to south—in order to ferret out rebels; it was a remarkable engineering feat completed with convict and imported Chinese labor. Off this main road, travel from mountain village to village was dangerous and difficult. Only twenty-one per cent of Puerto Rico's total area was under cultivation, including the mountain coffee plantations and the southern coast sugar plantations. Her farm production never equaled that of Martinique or Cuba.

Half of the island's budget of 1898 went to upkeep of the church and the navy. Nearly three times as much was spent on the church as on education. Eighty per cent of the population were illiterate. The majority of the people were abysmally poor. The thing that most shocked the American people when they first learned about Puerto Rico was that this great majority went barefoot; they did not even own a pair of shoes.

# 10 AMERICAN TAKEOVER

*"If there are a lot of Americans, run; if there are a few,
hide; if there are none, engage in battle."*
— *Alleged order of Spanish general in
Puerto Rico when the Americans landed*

In 1895, the Cuban poet-revolutionist, José Martí, was killed in
an unsuccessful rebellion against Spanish rule. General Weyler,
the new governor sent from Spain, clamped down on the Cuban
people with such brutality he won the nickname of Butcher
Weyler. Certain American sugar industrialists were distressed,
seeing their profits shrinking in the blood-stained, starving island.
William Randolph Hearst, editor of the *New York Journal*, upped
his newspaper's circulation by lurid accounts of Spanish atrocities
in Cuba.

On February 16, 1898, the United States battleship, *Maine*,
blew up and sank in Havana harbor. Hearst-indoctrinated Americans blamed the Spanish for the disaster, though their guilt was
never proven. President William McKinley did not want war with
Spain but yielded to public and Congressional pressure. The
Spanish-American War became official on April 24.

Puerto Rico felt the side effects a fortnight later. On May 12,
an American fleet under Admiral William Sampson sailed into
San Juan harbor and bombarded El Morro for 2 hours. Two unknown people were reportedly killed. One cannonball penetrated
13 feet within the outer wall of the fort, where it is still lodged.
Another shell went through the window of a jail cell where a
Spanish carpenter named Santiago Iglesias Pantín, a Socialist
labor leader, was being held. He had been organizing Puerto
Rican workers and urging them to ask for more wages. Under-

standably, he was unpopular with the authorities, who had jailed him again and again.

The American shell did not harm Iglesias. There was no further damage. After that 2 hours, the Americans sailed away.

In the heat of Cuba, some 17,000 American troops—wearing regulation heavy, blue woolen uniforms, half-sick with unfamiliar tropical diseases—fought a few battles with their unenthusiastic Spanish opponents. The Americans were obviously victorious over the Spanish by mid-July. In the meantime, Admiral Dewey had taken over the Spanish Philippines, which, with the island of Guam, was claimed by the American government as part of their spoils. And General Nelson Appleton Miles, Senior Commander of the United States Army, was given secret instructions to take Puerto Rico before Spain formally surrendered.

On July 25, 3 days after Spain presented a petition for peace through the French ambassador in Washington, Miles landed at Guánica—on Puerto Rico's southern coast—with some 3000 soldiers and sailors. Local people watched with curiosity rather than alarm as this stout general was hoisted ashore by his men. A few Puerto Ricans smiled and cheered. The Americans waved back weakly. Straight from Cuba, they were mostly sick with dysentery, and they were still in their hot uniforms. No Spanish garrisons were in evidence.

Three days later, General Miles joined General James Wilson, who had made an equally unopposed landing at nearby Ponce. From Ponce, Miles issued a proclamation which read in part:

In the prosecution of a war against the Spanish Crown, the people of the United States, inspired by the cause of liberty, justice, and humanity, have sent their armed forces to occupy the island of Puerto Rico. . . . The principal objective of the American military forces will be to put an end to the armed authority of Spain and give to the people of this island the greatest measure of liberty that may be compatible with military occupation.

For Puerto Rican liberals, the fine phrase about "liberty, justice, and humanity" did not quite offset the sinister sound of "military occupation." The more optimistic took on trust that their island would retain all the civil and political rights won from Spain in 1897 plus new benefits—and that they would soon be enjoying the same prosperity as the Americans.

In less than 3 months after the Americans landed, the Spanish government, staff, and troops moved out. On October 18, 1898, the Spanish colors were lowered and American flags were hoisted in San Juan. The island and its dependent islets were ceded to the United States on December 10, 1898, by a treaty signed in Paris.

In the meantime, Miles became the first American governor of Puerto Rico. Earlier in his career, he had been a celebrated Indian fighter in the Midwest. He viewed the Puerto Ricans much as he had the Apaches. Within weeks he was replaced by another military man, General John R. Brooke. Brooke confirmed the post of Luis Muñoz Rivera as prime minister and announced that the Puerto Rican constitution would remain in effect, with the proviso that their laws must be compatible with the United States Constitution.

The third American governor in 1898 was another general, Guy V. Henry, who was notoriously contemptuous of *all* civilians. At a meeting of the Puerto Rican parliament on December 19, 1898, General Henry announced he would favor elections by universal suffrage only when the United States decided that Puerto Ricans were "prepared for political responsibility." Muñoz Rivera resigned at this slap to his fellow countrymen, as did his cabinet. General Henry decided a new cabinet was not needed and filled important government posts with his own appointees. With one stroke, the Puerto Rican constitution was voided.

It was during these months that Americans began spelling the island's name as "Porto Rico," a mild insult which continued until 1932.

General George W. Davis replaced Henry as governor on August 15, 1899. He made it official that *all* government departments would be administered by his military appointees. "Reality does not correspond to the dream," commented Muñoz Rivera sadly. The Socialist Santiago Iglesias Pantín, who had expected no better, wrote on the "degrading and reactionary orders" put into effect "by the military advised by our own vested interests." It was true that the only Puerto Ricans the new rulers consulted seriously were the rich landowners. There were no discussions with political or labor leaders, nor was there any noticeable mating of minds between the American military governors and Puerto Rico's intellectuals and culturally elite.

Under Governor General Davis, the "Americanizing" of Puerto Rico got underway. The United States postal service was extended over the island. Puerto Rico money was abolished and American currency substituted. As it worked out, the transfer from Spanish pesos to American dollars meant a sharp wage cut for workers and a sharp increase in mortgages for coffee planters. It was decreed that henceforth all instruction in the newly launched public school system should be in English. This drastically slowed down the learning process for Spanish-speaking children. The favorite Puerto Rican sport of cockfighting was banned, as it had been off and on by their Spanish rulers. Whether it should be legal or not was on the official agenda for years. Since Puerto Ricans went right on matching their fighting cocks regardless of the law, the authorities finally gave up.

The military government was changed to a civil government under the provisions of the Foraker Act passed by the American Congress in 1900. Under this act, Puerto Ricans could elect a House of Representatives, but the governor, judges, commissioner of education, and other officials were appointed from Washington. The American Bill of Rights was guaranteed to Puerto Ricans, but they were not granted citizenship—which Spain had finally given them—and in other ways had less self-rule than under the charter negotiated with Spain by Luis Muñoz Rivera.

An important clause in the Foraker Act limited the amount of land any corporation could hold to 500 acres. This was designed as a safeguard to prevent large American companies from taking over the island's economy. The 500-acre law would be pointedly ignored.

Nothing in the Foraker Act prevented American companies

from exploiting Puerto Rican workers. American labor leader Samuel Gompers, visiting Puerto Rico in 1904, found men working 16 hours a day for forty cents, paid in stamps and redeemable only at the company stores of their American bosses.

It was in this same period that Santiago Iglesias, the labor leader, was sentenced to a 3-year imprisonment by a *Spanish* law that made it a crime to try to raise wages. His arrest caused such a cry of outrage in American labor circles that President Theodore Roosevelt revoked the sentence within the year.

# COLONY OF
# THE UNITED STATES

*"I saw children bitten by disease and on the verge of starvation, in slum dwellings — if you can call them dwellings — that make the hovels of Calcutta look healthy in comparison."*

　　　　　　　　　　*—John Gunther,* Inside Latin America

Beginning with the Foraker Act of 1901, civilian governors appointed from Washington moved in and out of beautiful La Fortaleza. With few exceptions, their appointments were rewards for some service to the political party in power. Few had any knowledge whatsoever of Caribbean affairs or could speak Spanish. More than a few carried their racial and national prejudices to their job. Puerto Ricans were "tropical people," one governor wrote home. They lacked the "stamina and initiative" to adjust to the "American way of life." That the Puerto Ricans were, in fact, more Spanish than anything else did not stop such men from treating them as inferior natives.

Luis Muñoz Rivera fought with Americans the same battle he had fought with the Spanish for greater self-rule, first as Puerto Rican Resident Commissioner in Washington and then as editor of a liberal paper in Washington. He died in 1916, frustrated and unhappy.

On March 2, 1917, Congress passed the Jones Act, which granted Puerto Ricans citizenship. By coincidence, perhaps, this measure made young Puerto Ricans eligible for the draft when America entered the First World War a month later. Before the end of the year, over 12,000 were called into service. A Puerto

Rican regiment was the first to be moved during the war; it was sent to the Canal Zone.

The Jones Act did not give Puerto Ricans any noticeable gains in self-rule. The attitude still prevailed that they were not yet ready to govern themselves.

American investors in sugar and tobacco poured into the island almost from the outset of American rule. One after another, hacienda owners sold out to them and moved away. By the early 1930's, four sugar corporations controlled 176,000 acres, making a travesty of the law limiting them to 500 acres. Because of the wide unemployment, they could keep wages at a starvation level. Workers in sugar cane, a seasonal industry, received about eight dollars a week (which the Brookings Institution in Washington estimated at twelve cents per day for each person in the family) during the season. For the several months when there was no work—called *tiempo muerto* (dead time)—they received nothing. Children were employed on the plantations at about $1.50 a week.

The old paternal relationship between hacienda owner and the workers vanished. The new boss, an absentee landlord, lived in America. No one ever saw him. He was represented by a foreman whose sole task was to increase production at the lowest possible cost. The land where workers had grown vegetables, raised a little livestock, or collected firewood was now plowed up to enlarge the plantations. Workers suspected of socialist leanings or of union organizing were discharged and blacklisted, often without knowing of what they were accused.

Outside the sugar plantations, salaries were even worse. Dock workers, truck gardeners, workers on coffee plantations received about $2.50 a week. In 1927, devastating hurricanes ruined most of the coffee plantations. Jobless and homeless, the workers migrated to wretched city slums.

The first American governor of Puerto Rico to show compassion for the people and respect for their heritage was Theodore Roosevelt, Jr., son of President Theodore Roosevelt, who served between 1929 and 1931. He opposed strongly the government policy of trying to remodel Puerto Ricans into continental Americans "in language, habits, and thoughts."

Unlike his predecessors, he felt it his duty to tour the mountain country to see how people lived. In an article called "Children of Famine," he described their plight: "Riding through the hills, I have stopped at farm after farm where lean, underfed women and sickly men repeated again and again the same story —little food and no opportunity to get more." As for babies, they were "little skeletons."

But following Governor Roosevelt's term, the situation grew worse instead of better. Under the Americans, the whole economy shifted from farming for direct consumption to growing crops for export. Thus, city people, and many country people as well, had to import food and clothing from America. The wretchedly poor were expected to pay New York or California prices for tools, textiles, shoes. Even most of their Caribbean neighbors were better off. A Puerto Rican was charged thirty cents a pound for meat; 45 miles away in Santo Domingo, meat cost six cents a pound. Most of the population never saw meat at all. Rice, beans, and codfish were the diet of the common man.

Although the United States had installed a health program, the ravages of disease throughout the island were appalling. In some villages, everyone had malaria. Tuberculosis and other diseases caused by malnutrition were widespread. There was no milk fit to drink. The public water supply in the cities was unsafe. Springs and streams of rural Puerto Rico were dangerous because of the parasite which causes the often fatal disease bilharziasis.

The most unspeakable conditions existed in the slums around San Juan, even on Puerto Rico's most beautiful beaches. "The houses have been built of odds and ends of wood; tottering and damp and rotted . . ." wrote newspaperwoman Martha Gellhorn. "You walk down paths in which rain stands, and the garbage stands."

In San Juan "wolf gangs" of city children pilfered and robbed and slept in parks, alleys, and hallways. Teenagers smashed post office mailboxes before witnesses, in the hope they would be sentenced to the federal reform school in Chillicothe, where they heard a boy would be fed, housed, clothed, and allowed to study English and master a trade.

Privately, government officials classified Puerto Rico as America's one great failure.

Inevitably there were Puerto Ricans who resented America's rule bitterly. The National Party appeared on the political scene; it advocated complete independence. Its leader was Pedro Albizu Campos, a dark-skinned mulatto. His wealthy father sent him to Harvard, where he graduated, brilliantly, with a law degree. In World War I, he served in a Negro regiment the duties of which were limited to manual labor. He was transferred to officers' training camp and became a lieutenant. The snubs he endured at Harvard and in the army because of his color turned him against the American domination. His fiery speeches constantly attacked American policy. In 1927, he was arrested in connection with a murder of a police chief in Washington and, more specifically, for conspiring to overthrow the United States government in Puerto Rico.

His followers organized a protest parade in Ponce for March 21, 1927. The Mayor of Ponce granted them permission, but Governor Blanton Winship, a southerner and a strong believer in military force to quell unrest, canceled their permit at the last moment. Rather than send their people home, the demonstrators voted to march anyway.

Little girls in starched white dresses and boys in white shirts and black trousers took their positions in the public plaza. Onlookers dressed in their best carried palm leaves for Easter Week. Although the plaza was ringed by some 150 police armed with automatic carbines, there was a holiday atmosphere. Suddenly, there were shots, followed by screams and more shots.

Fifteen demonstrators were killed that day, along with one bystander and two policemen; fifty were wounded. The governor's investigation committee blamed the demonstrators for the massacre, but the American Civil Liberties Union, after their investigation, reported there was no evidence that the demon-strators were armed and stated that the affair was "a brutal and unpardonable massacre of citizens by police."

Puerto Rico was one of the places which came under the scrutiny of Mrs. Eleanor Roosevelt, wife of President Franklin Roosevelt and America's most ardent crusader for justice. Her first trip was in 1934, and her special interest was the needlework industry.

The needlework industry was started theoretically as a philan-thropy to give women work at home. Fine linens were imported from Belgium with which Puerto Rican women made exquisitely embroidered lingerie, tablecloths, and garments, quickly showing amazing artistry in everything they did. Big industry took over with an elaborate system of contractors and subcontractors. Paid by piecework, the women received as little as one dollar a week and seldom more than three dollars. Mrs. Roosevelt was shocked by the rickety huts on stilts where these talented needleworkers lived, and even more so by the sight of tiny girls embroidering handkerchiefs to add a few pennies to the family income. On her return, she entreated President Roosevelt to do something to help the Puerto Rican people.

A few years later, President Roosevelt sent Rexford Tugwell, his Assistant Secretary of Agriculture, to the island. "Tell me whether we have got rid of the slums," he said, "and whether there is any place on the island to get a safe drink of water."

Tugwell returned to report that the water was filthy and was cut off half the time, even in San Juan. He also brought enlarged photos to show that the slums were as bad as ever. In 1941, Roosevelt sent him back, with the title of governor and instruc-tions to take what steps were needed. This was just after the United States Senate investigating committee had spent 10 days studying the misery of Puerto Rico, from which they concluded there was no solution to it.

# 12 OPERATION BOOTSTRAP

*"We learn by planting things in the mind that later bear fruit in understanding."*
— Luis Muñoz Marín

Luis Muñoz Rivera, the patriot of Barranquitas, had a son, Luis Muñoz Marín, born February 18, 1898, 2 days after the *Maine* blew up in Havana harbor. Much of his childhood was spent in Washington, D. C., where his father served as Resident Commissioner for Puerto Rico. At the time of his father's death, in 1916, young Luis was 18.

Greenwich Village, the artistic center of New York City, was his residence off and on for more than a decade. Like his father, he wrote poetry. Among his close friends were American poets William Rose Benét, Edward Arlington Robinson, and Sara Teasdale. One of his pastimes was translating English and American poetry into Spanish. Because of his wit and sharp intelligence, he became very popular in New York's literary and artistic circles.

Beneath the veneer of an easy-going sophistication, Muñoz Marín was passionately concerned about the unhappy fate of his people. To inform thinking Americans of the true state of affairs in Puerto Rico, he wrote articles for the liberal magazines, *The Nation* and *The New Republic,* and for H. L. Mencken's *The American Mercury.* He called himself a socialist, admired greatly the labor leader, Santiago Iglesias, who had succeeded Muñoz Rivera in the respectable position of Resident Commissioner for Puerto Rico. Muñoz also, at this time, firmly believed that the only hope for his country's salvation was independence.

In 1932, he was back in Puerto Rico, deep in politics—running on the ticket of the Liberal Party—winning the post of Senator-at-Large. Six years later, in 1938, he formed the *Partido Popular Democrático* (the Popular Democratic Party), whose members ever since have been called the *Populares*. The party's symbol was a jíbaro (mountaineer) in profile and wearing a *pava* (a large straw hat). The Party slogan was *Pan, Tierra, Libertad* (Bread, Land, Liberty). The Party platform called for enforcement of the 500-acre law, the promotion of local industry, land for landless farm workers, slum clearance, and better education; it did not mention liberty. Muñoz now felt that social reforms must take precedence over independence.

The Populares were penniless. Muñoz needed a chauffeur to take him on cross-country tours. Wryly, he asked a friend to find a man who did not want a salary, did not have to eat, and who could drive a car without gasoline.

In rural areas, it was the custom for politicians to pay people two dollars for their vote. Muñoz knew two dollars meant a lot of beans for a hungry family but he begged them to refuse. "Do you want two dollars or justice?" he asked them. "You cannot have both."

He made people admit that the men they had voted into power in the past had not improved their lot. He pointed out that if he was elected and did not live up to his promises, they could vote him out of power. This latter argument seems to have been the most effective. The Populares won the 1940 election by a narrow margin. Muñoz Marín became President of the Puerto Rican Senate.

When Rexford Tugwell became governor in 1941, he and Luis Muñoz worked closely together—usually in accord—toward the common aim of improving conditions. Those who had voted for Muñoz saw the results within a few months in minimum wage laws, child labor laws, and other social legislation.

By Muñoz' efforts, the 500-acre law was brought to a test. The United States Supreme Court upheld the Puerto Rican Supreme Court ruling that a certain sugar company holding 12,000 acres was violating the 500-acre law and should be fined and dissolved. By this decision, Americans finally realized that if Puerto Rico was to rise above the deep abyss of her poverty, her wealth could no longer be drained off by mainlanders.

The Second World War brought more acute hardship to add to the island's other troubles. Nazi U-boats in the Caribbean sank by the dozen American ships loaded with food and other necessities on which Puerto Ricans now depended. There were long bread lines and prices skyrocketed. Needlework and other local industries—except rum—collapsed for lack of transportation. Mrs. Tugwell, the governor's wife, set up milk kitchens to feed hungry children, enlisting the aid of wealthy Puerto Rican women. Their husbands followed the Spanish custom of keeping their wives at home; the women were delighted at the chance to get out in the world and be useful.

Certain conservative American senators were antagonized by Governor Tugwell's progressive measures; they were supported by the new Resident Commissioner in Washington for Puerto Rico, Bolivar Pagan; unlike his predecessors, he favored the big sugar interests. All their efforts to get Tugwell recalled failed flatly but after the war, he resigned. President Truman replaced him with the island's first Puerto Rican governor, Jesús T. Piñero. In 1947, the Jones Act of 1917 was amended to allow Puerto Ricans to elect their own governor.

The people's choice was Luis Muñoz Marín, who took office on January 2, 1949. Two years later, after two public referendums, Puerto Rico was proclaimed a commonwealth. As a commonwealth, the island would have the same freedom as any American state to run its internal affairs, yet would be under the military protection of the United States and would be entitled to various types of Federal aid. Puerto Ricans would not have to pay Federal income taxes, but could not vote in national elections and had no vote in Congress. The *Independistas* (Independents), led by Albizu Campos, were quick to point out that Puerto Rico was still in a humiliating position vis-à-vis the mainland and that the commonwealth was only a glorified colony. Muñoz Marín took the stand that it was a necessary step—not necessarily permanent

—to enable Puerto Rico to get desperately needed financial benefits.

By this time, he had launched his government on what became known as Operation Bootstrap. It was not quite a self-help project as the name implies. In essence, Operation Bootstrap was a plan to persuade American manufacturers to set up factories on the island, first by offering them tax exemptions over a specified period, and secondly, by convincing them they would have a plentiful supply of labor quite cheap—at least until the workers were ready to form strong unions and demand higher wages.

In 1950, Muñoz' government created FOMENTO (the Economic Development Administration) to advise prospective industries. They moved in, cautiously, about seventy the first year and then with increased momentum. Mostly in the field of light industry, they manufactured pharmaceutical supplies, women's wear, gloves, and shoes, to be sold on the mainland or in Puerto Rico as people earned enough to pay for them. The majority of the factory jobs the companies offered were for women. This caused some upset in family life, where the man had traditionally been the breadwinner. By 1968, Puerto Rico had 1700 manufacturing enterprises on its soil, nearly all American but a few from West Germany, France, England, and Japan, providing a total of 103,000 jobs.

A vast change took place on the island during this score of years, for which the new industries were only partially responsible. Massive doses of Federal aid were injected into the Puerto Rican economy in the form of grants, loans, and credits. Supplemented by Puerto Rican government funds, the aid was used for education, highways, welfare, and housing in which the most exciting and imaginative experiments were made.

All over the island community, building projects were set up. Men who had been living in dilapidated bohios could now donate 1 or 2 days a week to build themselves and their neighbors neat cement bungalows with such hitherto unknown conveniences as electricity and running hot and cold water. Their wives and children helped. The government donated technical guidance and loaned concrete forms, cement mixers, trucks. The only man on the project who received a salary was the foreman. The standard bungalow had two bedrooms, a bathroom, a living and dining room area and cost the new and happy occupants a mere $300. They could pay $20 down and $2.25 per month. It was their first introduction to installment buying.

For the indigent, the government built large apartment buildings at minimum but adequate standards, which rented according to income for a pittance. That even the poor had a right to decent housing was something that the predecessors of Governor Muñoz, Spanish or American, had never conceded.

For people with middle-class incomes, housing was available but expensive. The real estate industry boomed. A new high was reached in the Caribbean when a single Puerto Rican acre sold for over $30,000. In the high rise condominiums, a single apartment—very elegant to be sure—sold for $50,000 and upward.

The first luxury hotel in Puerto Rico was the Caribe Hilton, built on Condado Beach in San Juan in 1949—for something over $7 million—to provide visiting industrialists with the comfort they felt they had a right to expect. From the first year, the Caribe Hilton made money. A host of hotelmen rushed in to try their luck on the theory that if the Caribe Hilton could do it so could they.

In the Condado Beach area, beautiful old Spanish homes were razed to the ground, gardens were destroyed, magnificent old trees were uprooted to make room for the Borinquen, La Concha, Flamboyán, the Regency, Ritz of Condado, San Jerónimo, Da Vinci—all built on the premise that there was no end of rich Americans ready and willing to pay sixty dollars a day and upward. The era of Puerto Rico as America's tropical playground had opened full swing.

While granting that the million-dollar tourist industry could boost the island's economy, Governor Muñoz viewed this development unhappily. "We are not a nation of caterers," he said.

On the government's priority list was the providing of good water for the people. Not only was water in San Juan raised to acceptable standards. Hundreds of miles of pipelines or rural aqueducts brought pure and drinkable water to remote regions. Women, who once had traveled long distances with their pails and pitchers from streams and lakes, now had water in their homes or through a public tap. Pure water and better sanitation and hygiene were basic steps in fighting tropical diseases. Malaria almost disappeared. There were drastic drops in pneumonia and tuberculosis.

Literate Puerto Ricans had long known that the Americans' insistence on teaching Spanish-speaking Puerto Rican children in English was folly, but had been unable to change that policy. As late as 1939, a schoolteacher was dismissed because she spoke up frankly to the American Commissioner of Education about it. Under Governor Muñoz, the American experiment was dropped. Henceforth, children were taught in Spanish but with English as a second language. In 1939, about fifty-six per cent of school-age children—between 350,000 and 400,000—were not going to school because there were not enough schoolrooms. As new schools were built under Muñoz, literacy rose to a record ninety per cent. At the University of Puerto Rico, built in 1903, enrollment increased from 4000-plus in 1940 to over 30,000 in 1968, including the students in the new School of Medicine.

Puerto Rican women had been granted suffrage in 1932, but not until after the Populares came to power were there any women active in political life. One of a number who held important positions was Doña Felisa Rincón de Gautier, for many years the much-loved Mayor of San Juan. Doña Felisa, a hard-working gray-haired woman, had helped women get the vote and been active in helping to found the Popular Democratic Party. She had a way of getting people—from city engineers to garbage collectors —to work with her and for her in making San Juan a better place to live. On Three Kings Day, the "Twelfth Night" after Christmas, thousands of poor children with their parents assembled in Sixto Escobar Stadium to accept toys which Doña Felisa had collected from merchants or well-to-do families.

Regularly, she toured the San Juan slums, where people were

still living in windowless shacks without light or water and between which ran open rivers of sewers. Everyone knew her. Women sometimes kissed the hem of her skirt. They begged her to help them. More than anything else, she wanted to see the slums utterly destroyed, but there were not enough new buildings to replace them. People had to have homes. For the time being, she did what she could: getting expert construction men to help them rebuild their shacks more solidly, supplying new building materials when theirs were eaten by termites, giving them paint to brighten up their wretched dwellings.

Every Wednesday, Doña Felisa held a "day of interviews," when anyone—no matter how humble—could come and ask for help. At 9 A.M., she was at her desk. The petitioners were ushered in, one after another, to sit at her side for as long as they needed to tell her their problem. Some of the requests, such as shoes for children, could be handled quickly. Others were more complicated and had to be referred to various departments. Doña Felisa made it a point that every demand should be investigated and something done about it. One woman confided that her husband had been missing for 3 days. If Doña Felisa would come to dinner, she said, he would hear about it and return. The Mayor of San Juan accepted the invitation; the woman's husband came home.

Governor Muñoz worried lest Operation Bootstrap was giving his people too great a taste for material comforts. "What are we living for?" he demanded. "To beat the Russians? To own one automobile? Two, three, four?" To arouse his people's interest in more cultural things, he launched *Operación Serenidad* (Operation Serenity), which very loosely might be defined as the development of the arts and sciences. One project of Operation Serenity was the restoration of old Spanish colonial mansions. Another was the *Teatro Rodante* (the roving theatre) sponsored by the University of Puerto Rico, which brought actors and their plays in trailer trucks from town to town. The annual Pablo Casals Musical Festivals are part of Operation Serenity, as are the archeological researches of the Institute of Puerto Rican Culture. There are no statistics as to whether the average Puerto Rican would be willing to give up his automobile, or automobiles, for art, but at least the government had not neglected that side of his education.

Luis Muñoz Marín was re-elected as governor in 1952, 1956, and 1960. In 1964, he withdrew in favor of a colleague, Robert Sánchez Vilella, who won by a small margin. There was a split in Muñoz' Popular Democratic Party before the 1968 elections. The dissidents called themselves the People's Party. Although these two parties both favored the commonwealth and together received over sixty per cent of the votes, because of the split, the election was lost to the New Progressive Party, who supported statehood and Luis Ferré, the cement tycoon from Ponce. The *Partido Independentista Puertorriqueño* (the Independence Party) won only about three per cent of the total, which understandably caused almost everyone to dismiss them as of no importance.

The record of achievement of the Populares during their 20 years in power was more than impressive. Per capita income increased from $122 annually in 1940 to $1123 in 1968, the highest in the Caribbean. Among factory workers and employees, average pay jumped from $1706 a year in 1950 to more than $5900 in 1968. The factory owners were loud in their praise of the learning ability and skill of their Puerto Rican workers. It was true that nearly all the managerial and executive jobs in the new industries were held by non-Puerto Ricans, and workers' salaries were so low compared to the mainland that thousands left to seek jobs there.

Life expectancy increased from 61 years in 1948 to 70.2 in 1968, comparing favorably to 70.5 in mainland United States. The annual death rate per 1000 population shrank from 11.4 in 1948 to 6.07 in 1968, considerably lower than the 9.4 per 1000 in continental United States.

From being the national disgrace of the United States, Puerto Rico had become the showplace of the Western World. Heads of Latin American governments and of the new African nations and other Third World leaders from as far away as Borneo visited the island to find out the secret of Puerto Rico's prosperity. Critics, greatly outshouted, hinted that all was not perfect in this utopia. The per capita income was still little more than half that of Mississippi, the poorest state of the mainland. Income from agriculture was shrinking rather than rising which was wrong in a country where agriculture was the chief natural resource. Most damning of all, in spite of increase in population, unemployment remained at an average of eleven per cent, less in San Juan, more in some rural areas, but too much everywhere.

# 13 THE QUESTION MARKS

*"A man must do three things during his life: plant a tree, write a book, and have a son."*
— *Puerto Rican saying*

Modern Puerto Rico is a series of question marks.

For those who love the island poinsettias and who sorrow for the vanishing parrots in the woods and for the loss of the great hardwood forests of pre-Columbian times, the most important question is about ecology.

Will the evil by-products of industrialization, the ugly scars on the land and the pollution of the air, spread out like giant fungi in the senseless way they have done on the mainland? Will the dedicated conservationist groups win out over the "vested interests"—the name given to those individuals or corporations whose sole interest is in making money, no matter what harm is done to the land and the people?

There is the case of the two American copper companies who wanted to build a smelter next to Guanica National Forest on the south coast. An advisory council investigating the matter for the government predicts that emissions from the smelter of 70 tons of sulfur dioxide gas per day would endanger the rich flora and fauna of the forests.

There is the case of Phosphorescent Bay, near Parguera, the home of the remarkable dinoflagellates which sparkle when anything disturbs them. Now, the dinoflagellates of this bay, one of four similar ones in the Western Hemisphere, are threatened by industrial waste from nearby petroleum refineries.

Will Puerto Rico's Environmental Quality Board, created to

protect the island's scenic treasures, have the proper authority to act when such threats arise?

And what about the dreary business section of modern San Juan and "modernized" sections of other old towns? The parking lot where there were once trees and grass? The garish neon lights advertising something or other? Will these eyesores multiply?

There are men in the government deeply concerned with city planning. There are superb Puerto Rican architects, a profession for which they seem especially gifted. In planning new suburbs for beauty, convenience, and comfort, will they be able to win out over the "vested interests"?

A burning question for the young men of Puerto Rico is the war in Vietnam, as unpopular there as on the mainland. Can Puerto Ricans be forced to serve when, as members of the commonwealth, they have no Federal vote? In March 1971, the students of the University of Puerto Rico staged a demonstration against the presence of the Reserve Officers Training Corps for the purpose of on-campus recruiting. The police arrived. Three persons were killed, more than sixty injured, sixty-four arrested. Governor Ferré blamed everything on "a cadre of Communists trained in Cuba." Nonetheless, the "image" of Puerto Rico as a happy people, forever grateful to the mainland, was severely tarnished.

How to stop student unrest is just one of the troublesome questions which faced Governor Ferré. What was to be done about crime? Juvenile delinquency, drug use, petty thefts, grand larceny have appeared on the island, not in epidemic quantity but bad enough. The new bungalows in the city and suburbs have iron grillwork in fanciful patterns like lace curtains—covering the porch, the door, the entrance to the garage—for protection from robbers. It is, at times, no longer safe for a woman alone to walk the streets of San Juan at night.

How can one make more jobs? Unemployment, after Ferré became governor in 1968, rose to thirteen per cent. The depression on the mainland was generally blamed. Some factories closed down, causing more layoffs. The long East Coast dockworkers' strike held up transportation of factory products to the mainland and of consumer goods to Puerto Rico, bringing scarcity and higher prices.

Governor Ferré, who, as an industrialist, thought in terms of stocks and bonds, proposed a scheme to aid the "sagging economy"—to sell preferred stock to the people, financed through unsecured bank loans. Any Puerto Rican earning between $500 and $7800 annually would be allowed to purchase the stock. There would be guarantees against loss. He found few supporters for his scheme, however.

The hotel men of Puerto Rico have their questions too. Why are so many of their splendid hotels half empty? What has happened to all those rich American tourists with their dollar-filled wallets? Are they so fickle that in spite of the enticements Puerto Rico offers they have taken vacations elsewhere—in London, Paris, the Riviera, Acapulco, Borneo?

By government figures, there were 512,000 hotel guests in 1970 and 471,000 in 1971, a drop of more than eight per cent. Many of these came on "package deals" of the sort that include jet fare, four nights in a luxury hotel, and a free cocktail—all for $169 or some other minimal sum. Money spent by tourists dropped by more than eleven per cent.

Some well-to-do visitors now rent elegantly furnished apartments in condominiums rather than stay at a hotel. Not only do they save money, they have more privacy and more space. More sophisticated and less money-loaded tourists go to guest houses, usually old Spanish mansions remodeled with private baths. The beaches that face them are just as white and their patios as decorated with tropical plants as in the big hotels, but the atmosphere is more informal. The staff is more friendly. The guests, who may include poets, writers, artists, students—from Europe as well as the mainland—are more interesting.

To prevent the hotels from closing down, the government has bought up one after another, including the famous El Convento in Old San Juan, a remodeled convent, and launched a 1-million dollar advertising campaign to attract more visitors. Will this prove a success? Privately, a government official admits that "the luxury market is a very limited market."

The biggest question mark in Puerto Rico today is its political future. In the November 1972 elections, the Popular Democratic Party made a comeback. Ferré and his New Progressive Party were defeated by Rafael Hernandez Colon of the Populares. Temporarily, at least, Ferré's ambition of transforming Puerto Rico into the 51st state in the United States was blocked. The vote would indicate that for the time being most Puerto Ricans prefer the tax-free status of the Commonwealth to statehood. Puerto Rico's ultimate destiny remains as nebulous as ever.

Puerto Ricans have acquired a host of new skills under the American influence: in building, in manufacturing, in practically every field. They have also picked up some economically unsound American customs, such as installment buying. Everything is bought on time. Along Ponce de León Avenue, store after store carries a sign urging customers to come inside to discuss "*nuestro* [our] layaway plan." Hot dogs and hamburgers have infringed on the more nourishing and vitamin-filled Puerto Rican dishes. Coca Cola and pop drinks too often substitute for native orange or pineapple juice. There are other, more subtle, American influences; some hold they have resulted in a lowering of cultural and aesthetic standards.

Is there any chance that Puerto Rico will ever wrench itself free from its American apron strings and make a stab of running its own affairs as a free and independent nation?

In spite of all predictions to the contrary, and in spite of its poor showing in elections, there is evidence that the Independence Party is growing. Most of its members are young. Many are university students. They are idealistic, determined and romantic. They are notably unfair to Luis Muñoz Marín, whom they consider to have sold out to American imperialists. To be sure, not very many of them are old enough to remember the pre-Muñoz days when hunger, poverty, and disease stalked the land like three macabre sisters. The *Independistas* have their own newspaper, *Claridad* (clarity), which is highly competent and gives information glossed over or ignored in other newspapers. Every so often, their headquarters or newspaper offices are raided. The police have shown little inclination to protect them. To be an Independista today is considered as radical, as traitorous even, as was Muñoz Rivera's Autonomist Party in 1887, which advocated self-government and a dominion status in relation to Spain.

Because being an Independista is considered not quite respectable, many people who secretly sympathize with them do not come out for them openly. The Independents themselves claim that many of their members refused to vote because they considered it a waste of time. So no one knows exactly how strong they are.

There are also liberals who sincerely think that colonialism is wrong and that Puerto Rico is still in effect a colony, but who have doubts about how an independent Puerto Rico could survive. How ever could this overpopulated island exist without American aid and American industry? One long-time Independista says the Puerto Ricans would simply have to return to an agricultural economy, to live off the land as the Indians did. Were they not healthy and happy before the Spaniards came? The idea of returning to nature is appealing, but unrealistic, as nearly everyone would admit. No way has yet been found to turn the clock backward.

A thousand reasons can be mustered why independence for Puerto Rico is impossible. But what if the people decided to take the gamble anyway? What if they decided that, in spite of all obstacles, they wanted a chance to try and make it on their own? If, when, and how they achieved independence, would they adopt the Old Indian name of Boriquén?

# BIBLIOGRAPHY

Aitken, Thomas, Jr., POET IN THE FORTRESS, LUIS MUÑOZ MARÍN. New York: New American Library, 1964.

Alegría, Ricardo E., DESCUBRIMIENTO, CONQUISTA Y COLONIZACION DE PUERTO RICO, 1493–1599. San Juan: Coleccion de Estudios Puertorriqueños, 1971.

Baldwin, Leland Dewitt, THE STORY OF THE AMERICAS. New York: Simon and Schuster, 1943.

Brameld, Theodor, THE REMAKING OF A CULTURE, LIFE AND EDUCATION IN PUERTO RICO. New York: Harper & Row, 1959.

Calitri, Princine, COME ALONG TO PUERTO RICO. Minneapolis, Minn.: T. S. Denison & Co., 1971.

Chenault, Lawrence, THE PUERTO RICAN MIGRANT IN NEW YORK CITY. New York: Columbia University Press, 1938. Reissued with a new foreword by F. Cordasco. New York: Russell & Russell, 1970.

Cordasco, Francesco, Castellanos Diego, and Bucchioni, Eugene, PUERTO RICANS ON THE UNITED STATES MAINLAND: A Bibliography of Reports, Texts, Critical Studies, and Related Materials. Totowa, N.J.: Rowman & Littlefield, 1972.

Cordasco, Francesco, and Bucchioni, Eugene, THE PUERTO RICAN EXPERIENCE: A Sociological Sourcebook. New York: Littlefield & Adams, 1972.

——— THE PUERTO RICAN COMMUNITY AND ITS CHILDREN ON THE MAINLAND: A Sourcebook for Teachers, Social Workers and Other Professionals. Metuchen, N.J.: Scarecrow Press, 1972.

Fitzpatrick, Joseph, P., PUERTO RICAN AMERICANS: THE MEANING OF MIGRATION TO THE MAINLAND. Englewood Cliffs, N.J.: Prentice-Hall, 1971.

Gruber, Ruth, PUERTO RICO, ISLAND OF PROMISE. New York: Hill & Wang, 1960.

Gunther, John, INSIDE LATIN AMERICA. New York: Harper & Row, 1941.

Hancock, Ralph, PUERTO RICO, A SUCCESS STORY. Princeton, N.J.: D. Van Nostrand, 1960.

Hanson, Earl Parker, PUERTO RICO, LAND OF WONDERS. New York: Alfred A. Knopf, 1960.

Lewis, Gordon K., PUERTO RICO, FREEDOM AND POWER IN THE CARIBBEAN. New York: Harper & Row, 1963.

Lewis, Oscar, LA VIDA, A PUERTO RICAN FAMILY IN THE CULTURE OF POVERTY—SAN JUAN AND NEW YORK. New York: Random House, Inc., 1965.

Mayerson, Charlotte, L., TWO BLACKS APART. New York: Holt, Rinehart & Winston, 1965.

Mintz, Sidney W., WORKER IN THE CANE. Story of Anastacio (actually Eustaquio) Zayas Alvarado, called Don Taso. New Haven, Conn.: Yale University Press, 1960.

Mixer, Knowlton, PORTO RICO, HISTORY OF CONDITIONS SOCIAL, ECONOMIC, POLITICAL. New York: Macmillan, 1926.

Morison, Samuel Eliot, ADMIRAL OF THE OCEAN SEA. Boston: Little, Brown and Company, 1942.

Morison, Samuel Eliot, and Obregón, Mauricio, THE CARIBBEAN AS COLUMBUS SAW IT. Boston: Little, Brown and Company, 1964.

Padilla, Elena, UP FROM PUERTO RICO. New York: Columbia University Press, 1958.

Page, Homer, PUERTO RICO, THE QUIET REVOLUTION. New York: Viking Press, 1963.

Petrullo, Vincenzo, PUERTO RICAN PARADOX. Philadelphia: University of Pennsylvania Press, 1947.

Rand, Christopher, THE PUERTO RICANS. New York: Oxford University Press, 1958.

Rodman, Selden, THE CARIBBEAN. New York: Hawthorn Books, Inc., 1968.

Ruiz, Belvis Segundo, Acosta, José, Julian and Quiñones, Francisco Mariana, PROYECTO PARA LA ABOLICION DE LA ESCLAVITUD EN PUERTO RICO. San Juan: Institute of Puerto Rican Culture, 1959.

Soler, Luis M., HISTORIA DE LA ESCLAVITUD NEGRA EN PUERTO RICO (1493–1890) San Juan: University of Puerto Rico, 1970.

Tugwell, Rexford Guy, THE STRICKEN LAND, THE STORY OF PUERTO RICO. New York: Doubleday & Company, Inc., 1947.

Turnbull, David, CUBA; WITH NOTICES OF PORTO RICO AND THE SLAVE TRADE. London: Longman, Orme, Brown, Green, and Longman, 1840.

Van Deusen, Richard James, PORTO RICO, A CARIBBEAN ISLE. New York: Henry Holt and Company, 1931.

Vivas, José Luis, HISTORIA DE PUERTO RICO. New York: Las Americas Publishing Co., 1962.

Young Lords Party and Abramson, Michael, PALANTE YOUNG LORDS PARTY. New York: McGraw-Hill Book Company, 1971.

Works Project Administration, PUERTO RICO, A GUIDE TO THE ISLAND OF BORIQUEN. Sponsored by the Puerto Rico Department of Education. New York: The University Society, Inc., 1940.

# INDEX

## ABOUT THE AUTHOR

Robin McKown was born in Denver, Colorado and spent her summers in the Rocky Mountains. A graduate of the University of Colorado, she studied at Northwestern University School of Drama and at the University of Illinois. Before writing any books, she wrote one-act plays, one of which was produced. Her book, JANINE, received a Child Study Association award and was chosen, along with another of her books, HEROIC NURSES, as a Junior Literary Guild selection. She is also the author of THE CONGO, and THE AMERICAN REVOLUTION: THE FRENCH ALLIES.